INTRODUCTION

Have a few minutes?

Whether you have a few minutes to relax or a few hours to fill, this coloring books is for you!

Page after page of one-of-a-kind mandalas were designed with your free time in mind. Some pages are more complex, some are simpler, pick and choose which you want to do in the amount of time you have.

Each page is specifically designed to be one sided so you don't have to worry about losing any artwork if you want to take the pages out and frame them. Also each page does not go to the edges so that you can color over by the spine without any hassles!

You have my permission to photocopy the images for personal use only.

Whether you like to color in front of the TV for a few hours or have fifteen minutes to fill before picking up the kids this coloring book has something for all.

Art should be fun and relaxing, so go crazy!

Enjoy!
♥ Meredith

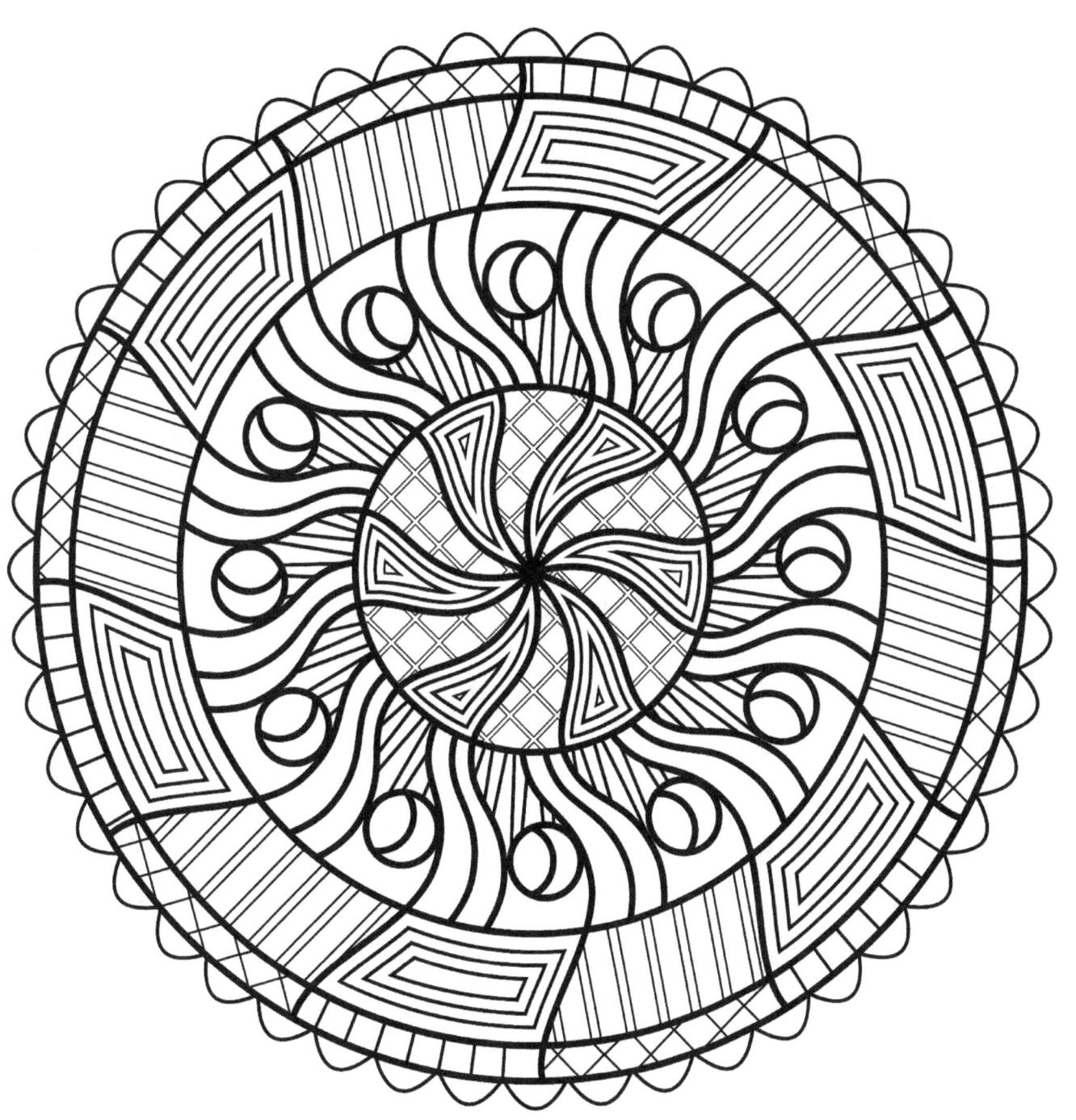

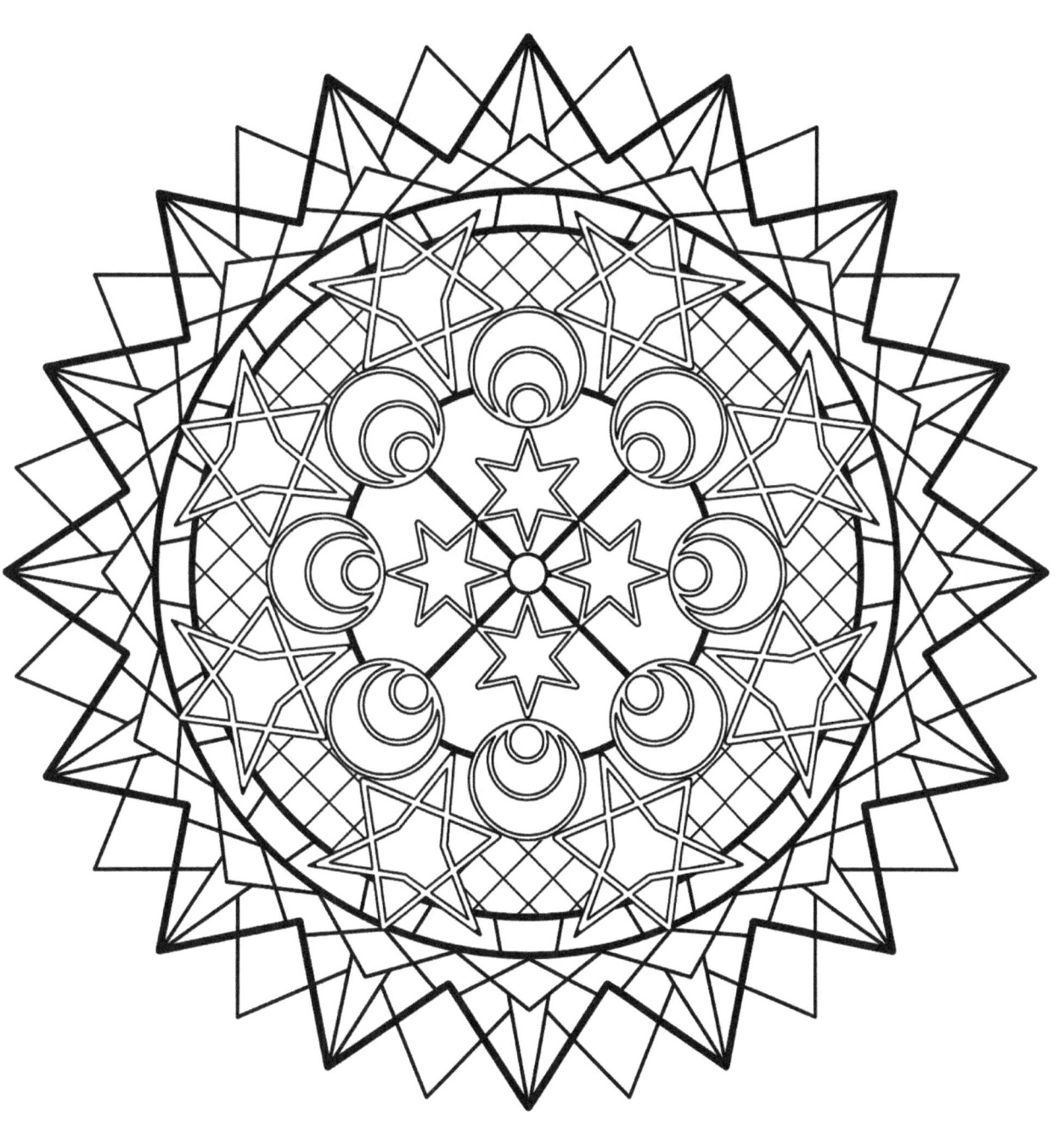

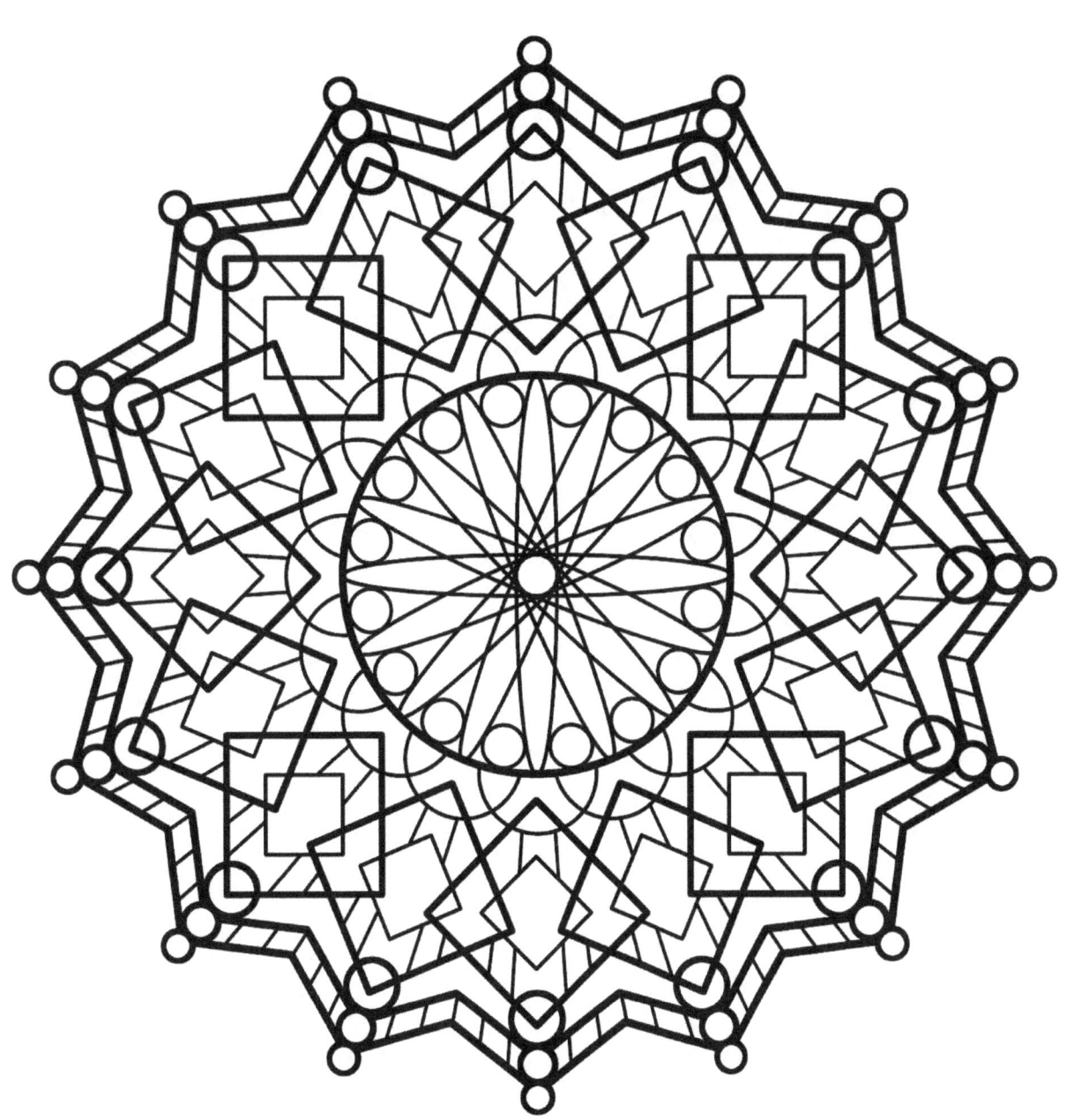

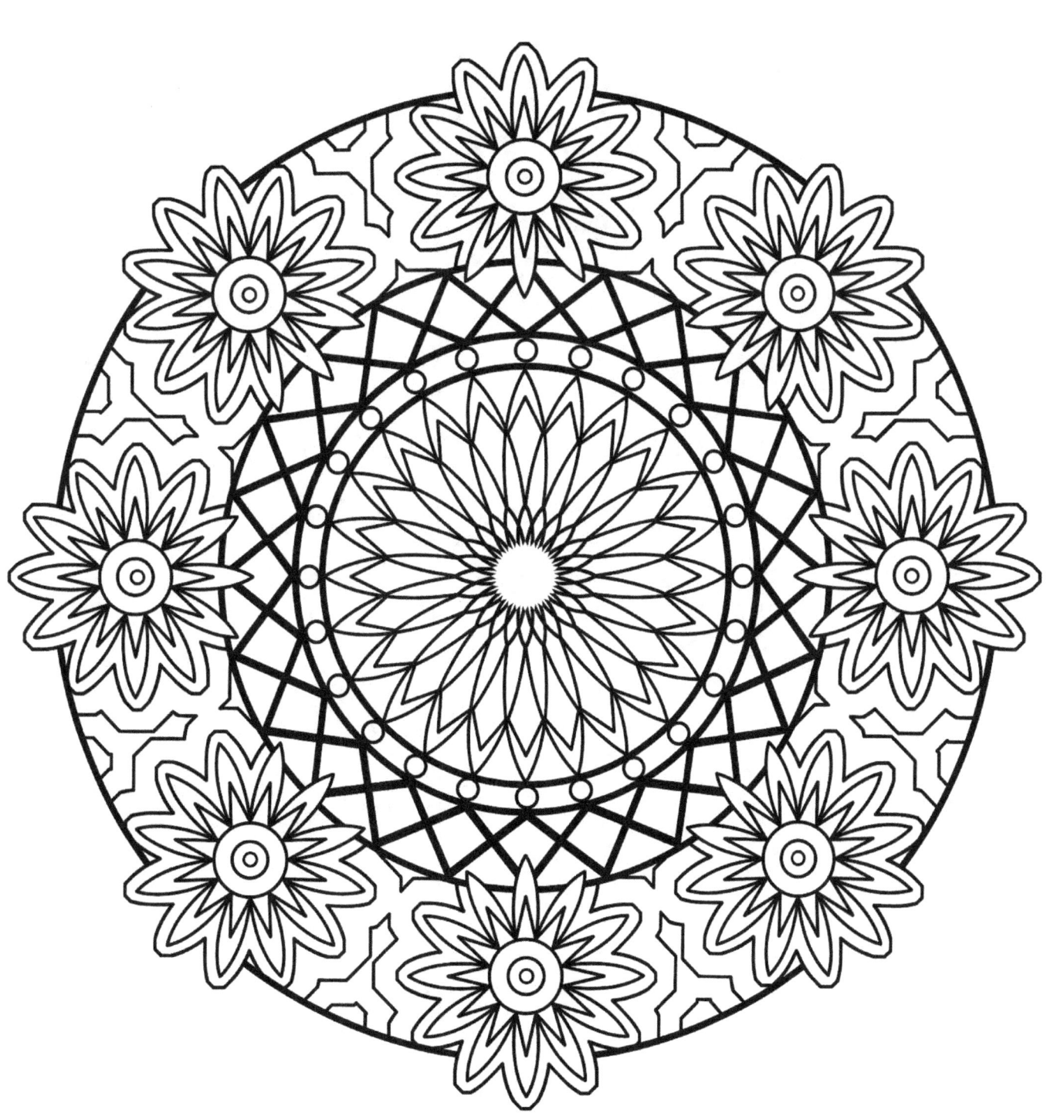

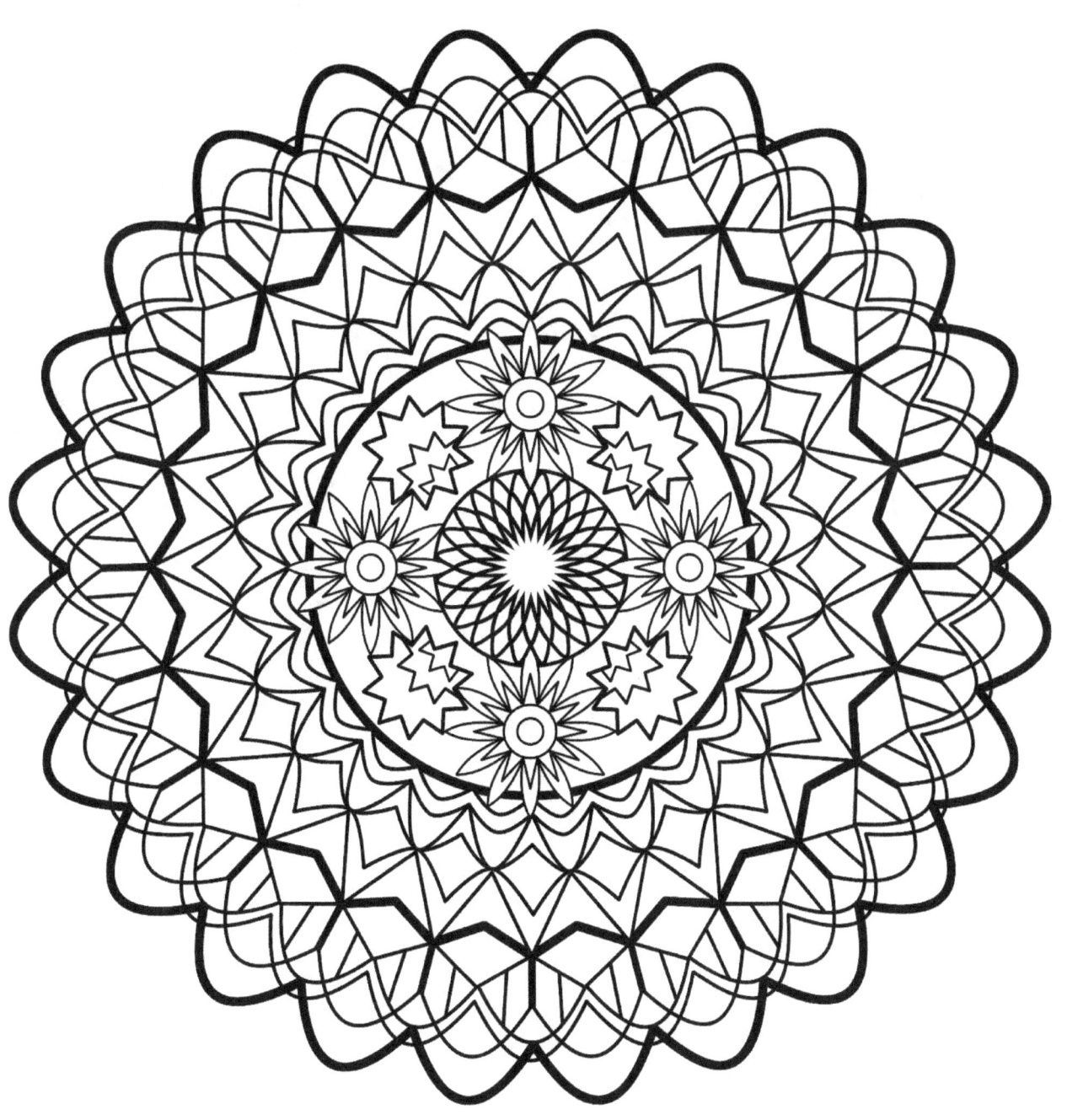

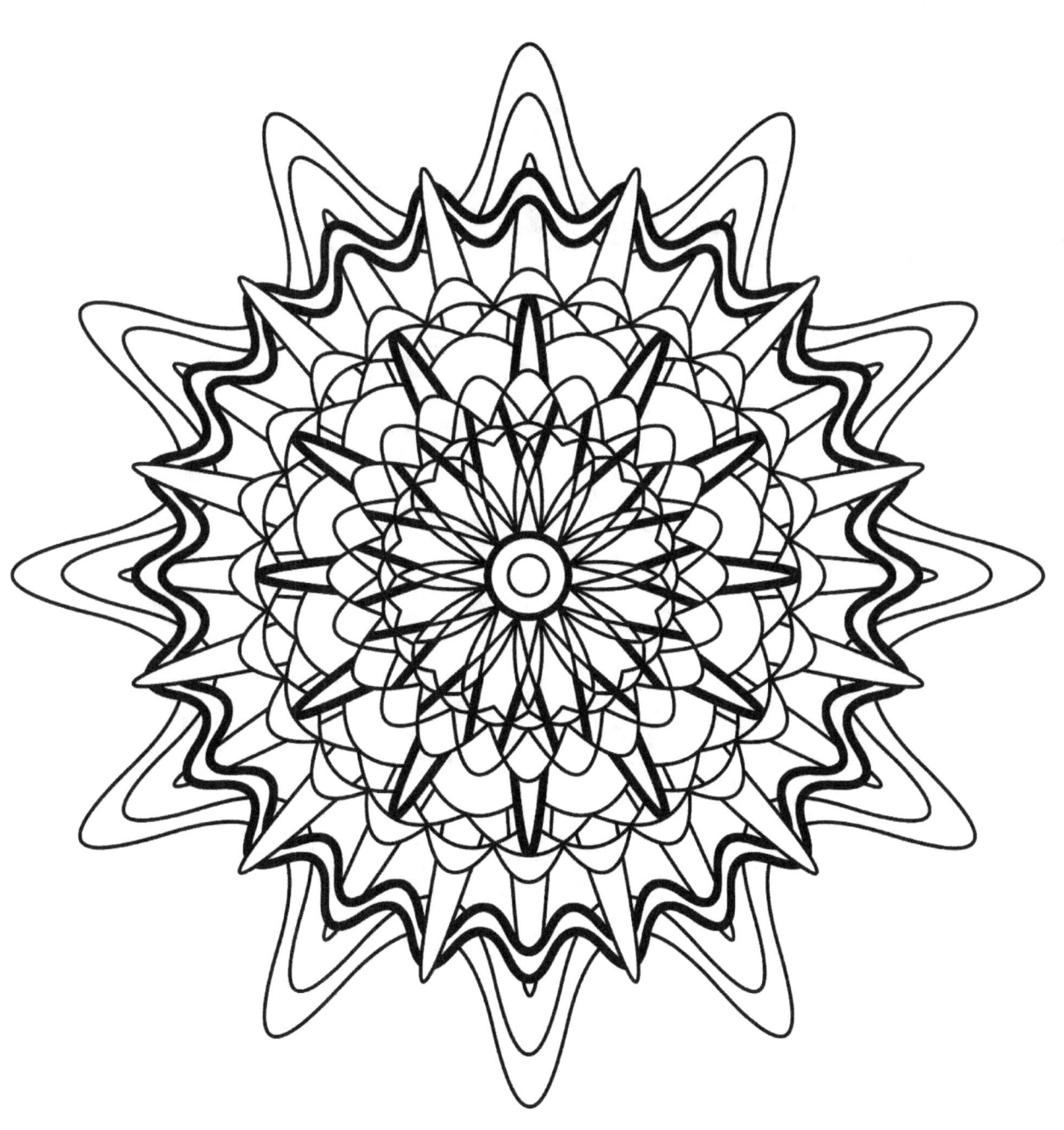

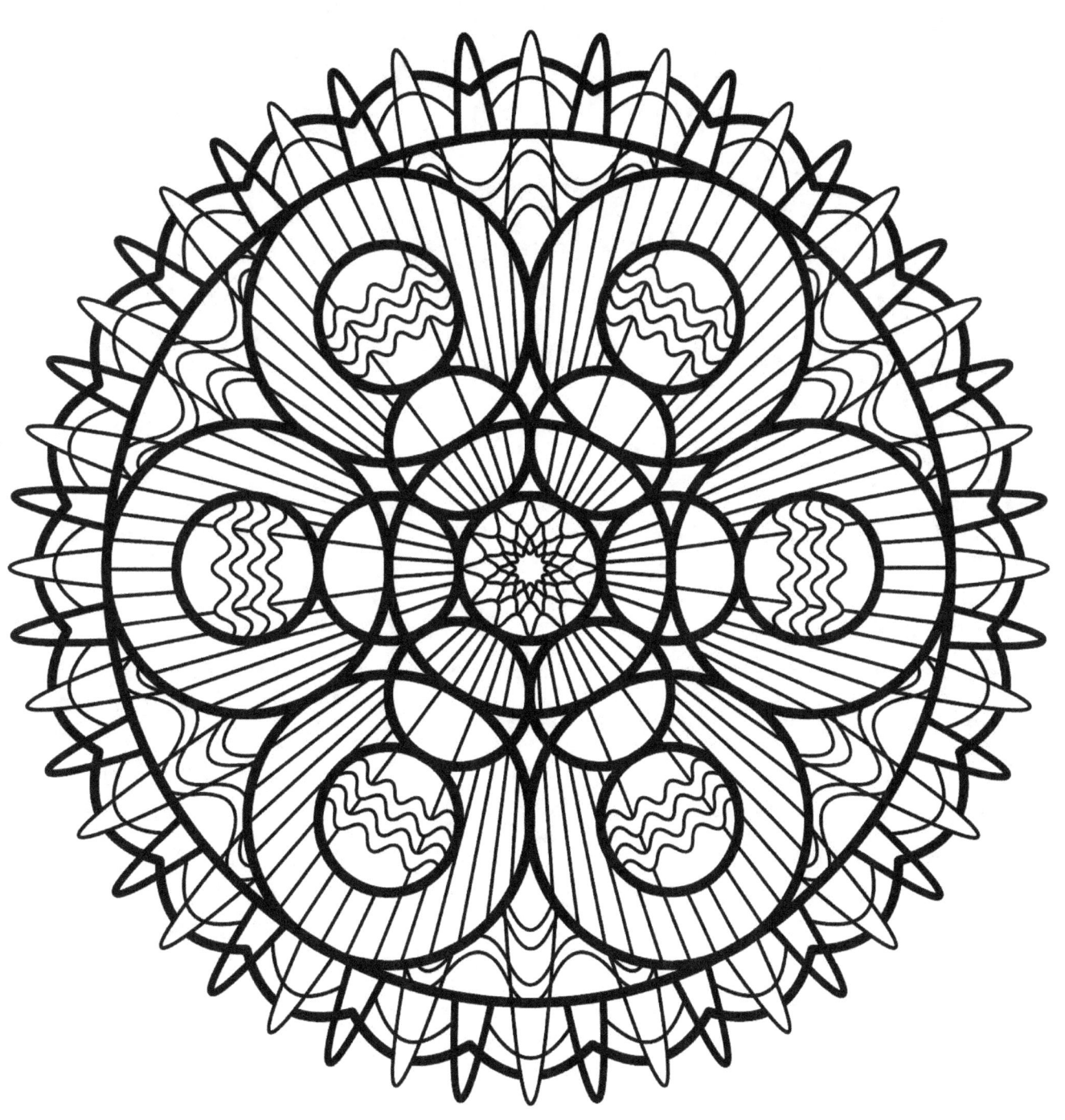

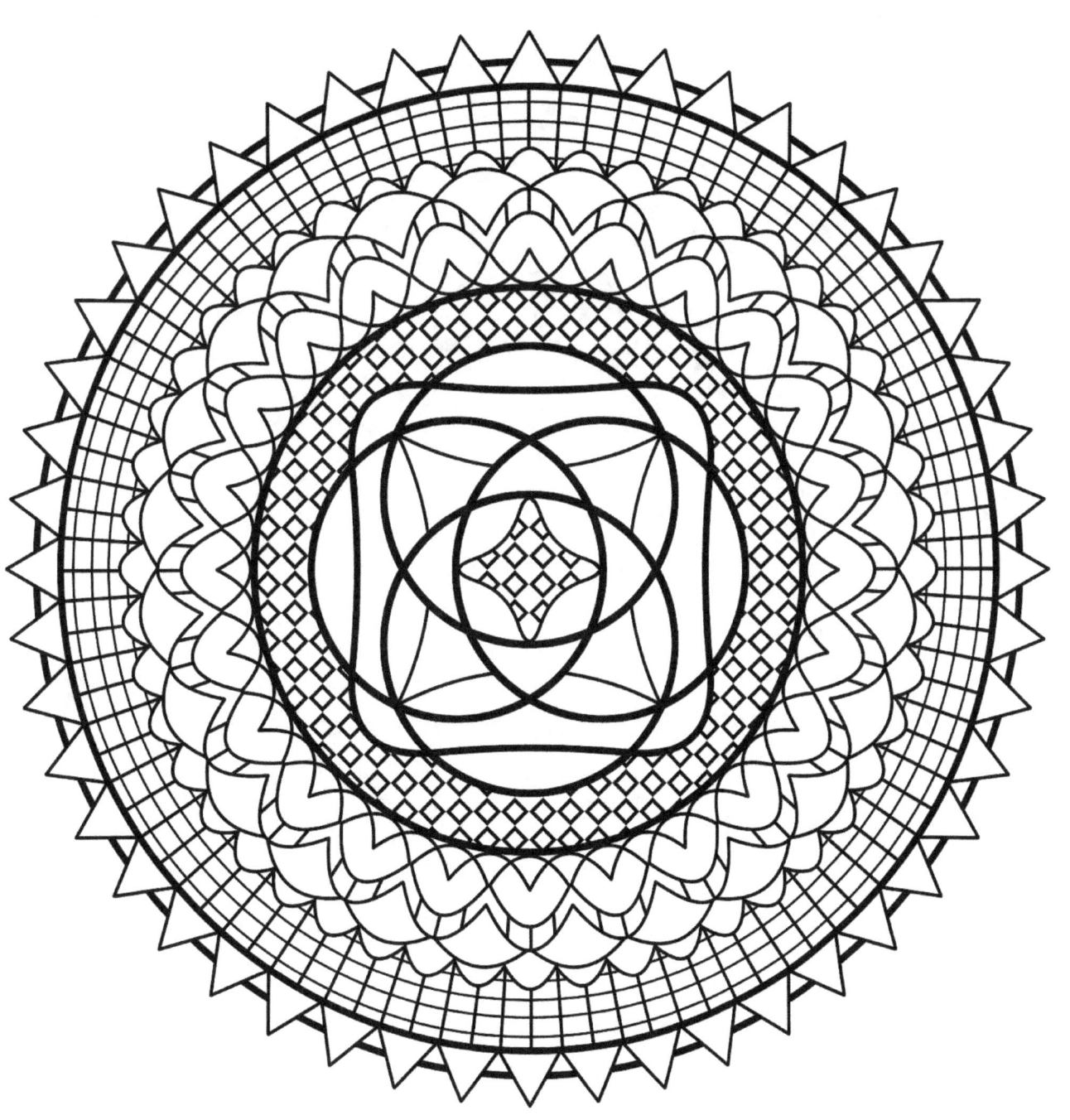

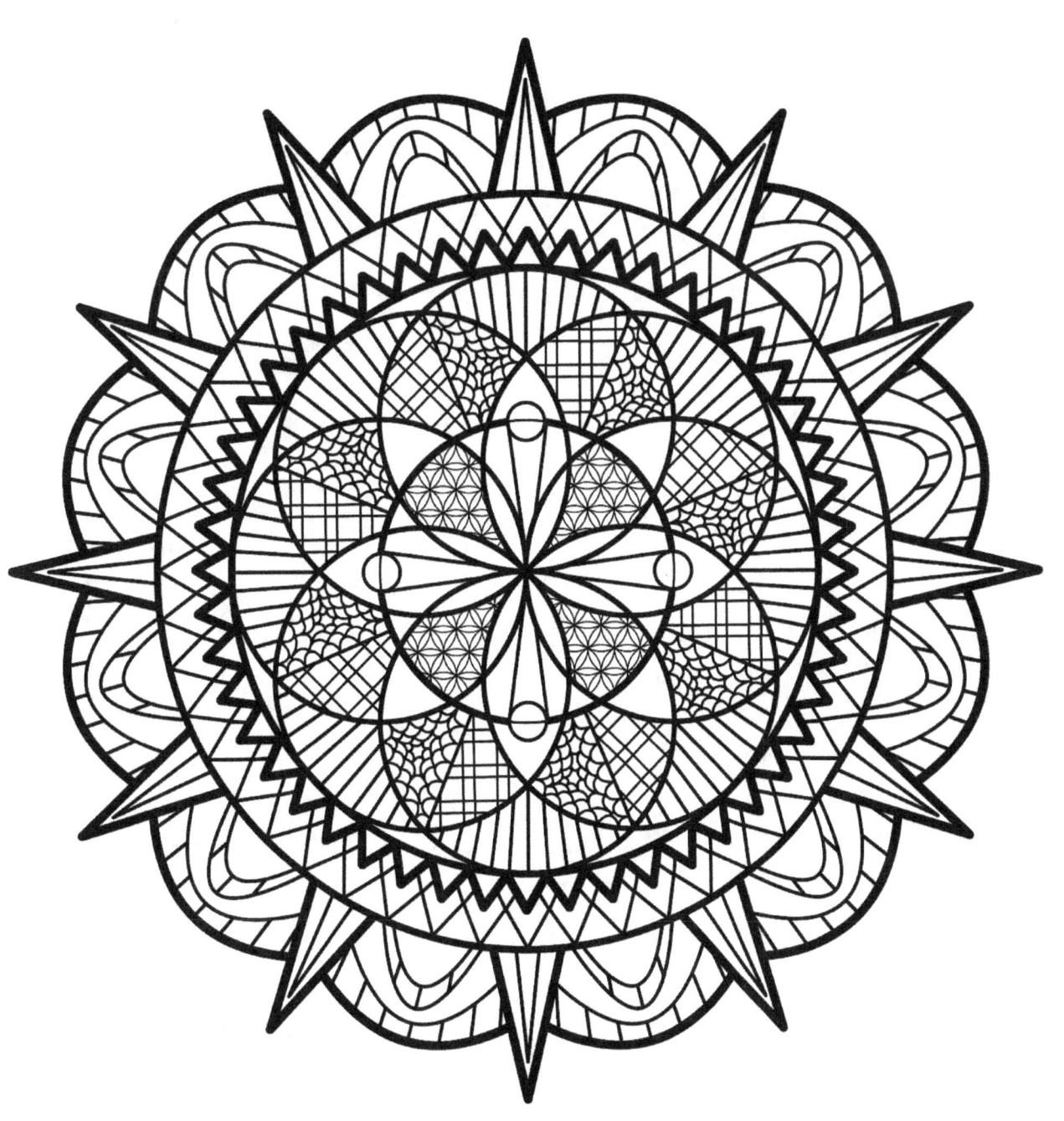

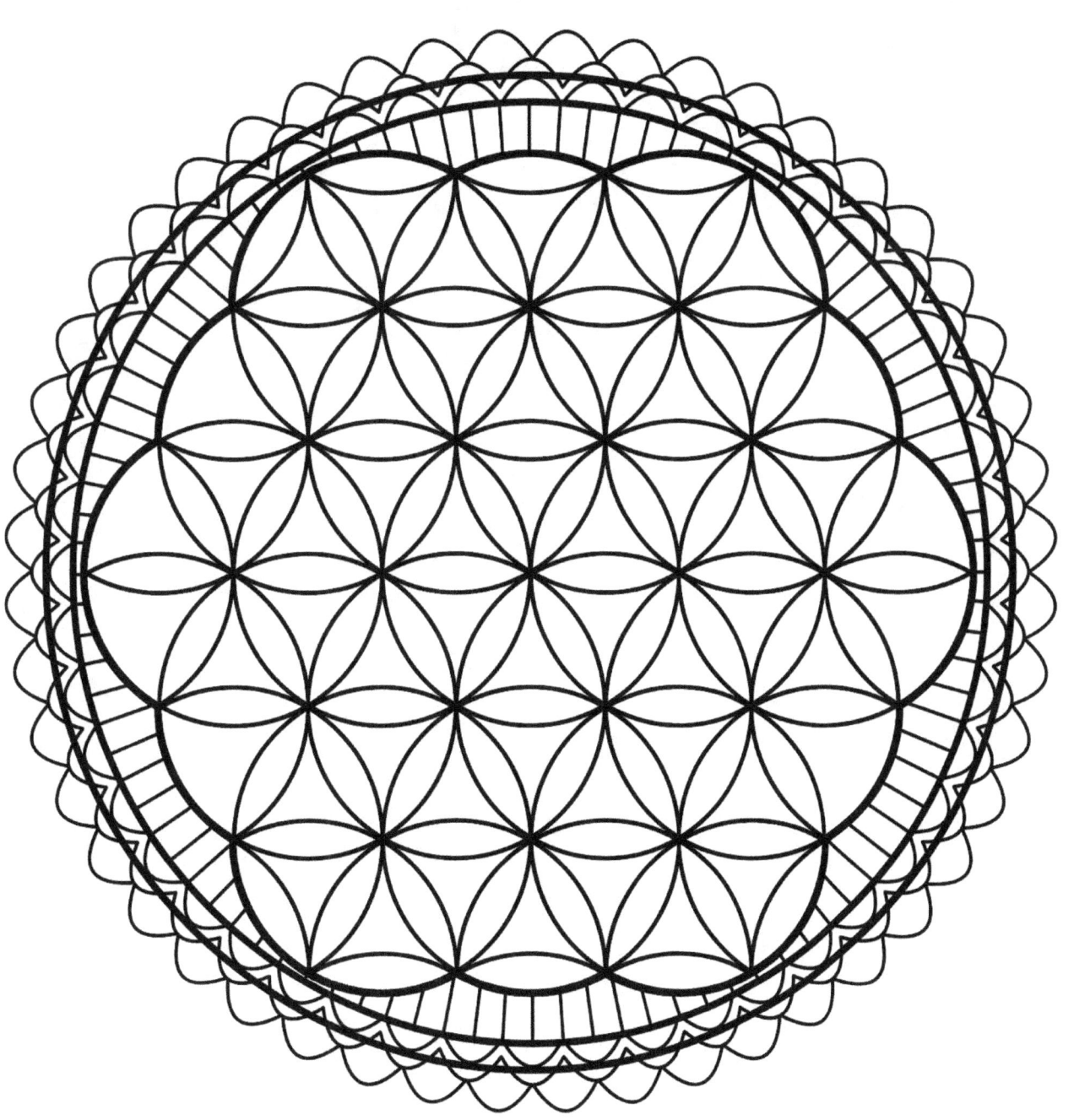

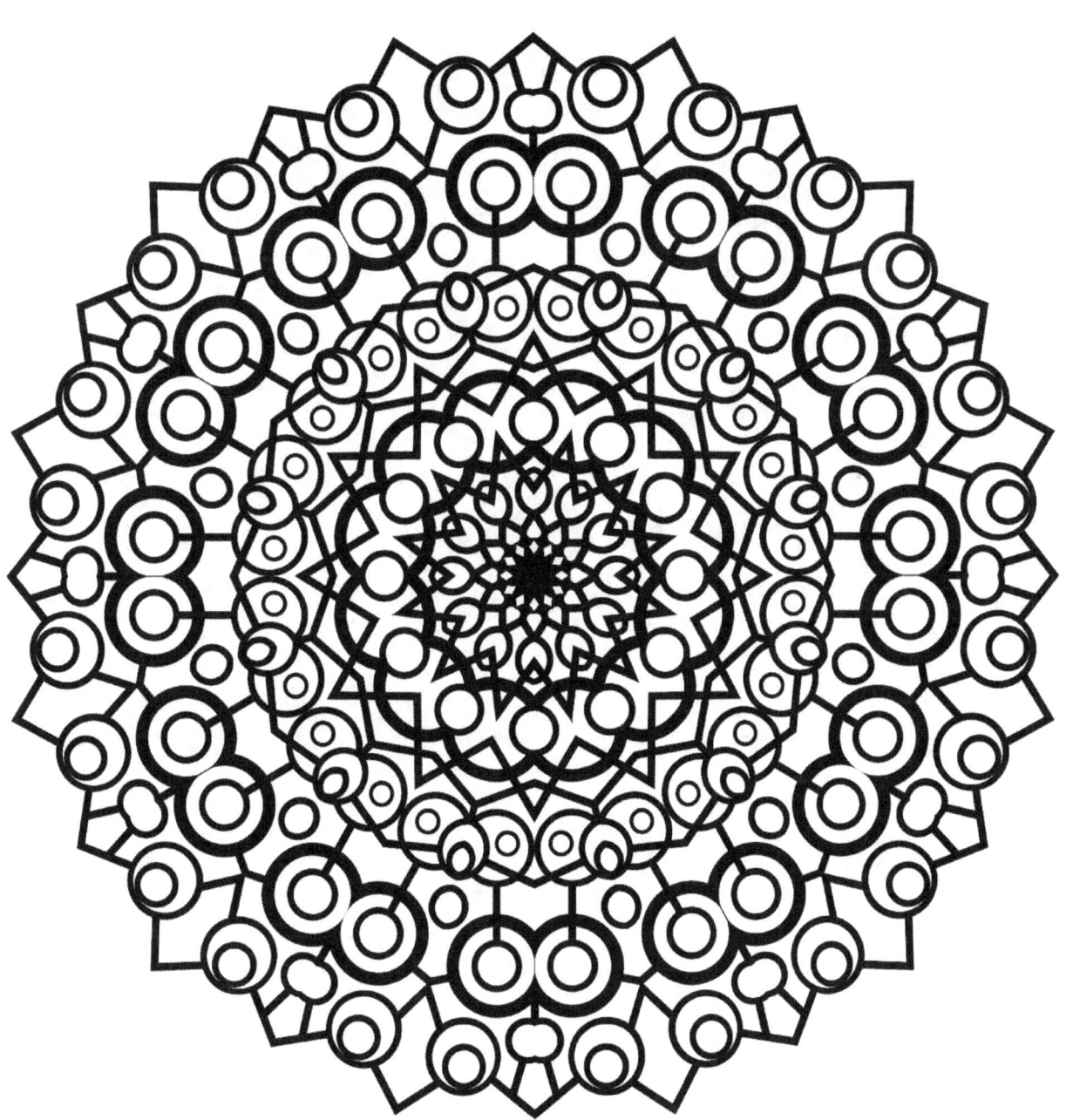

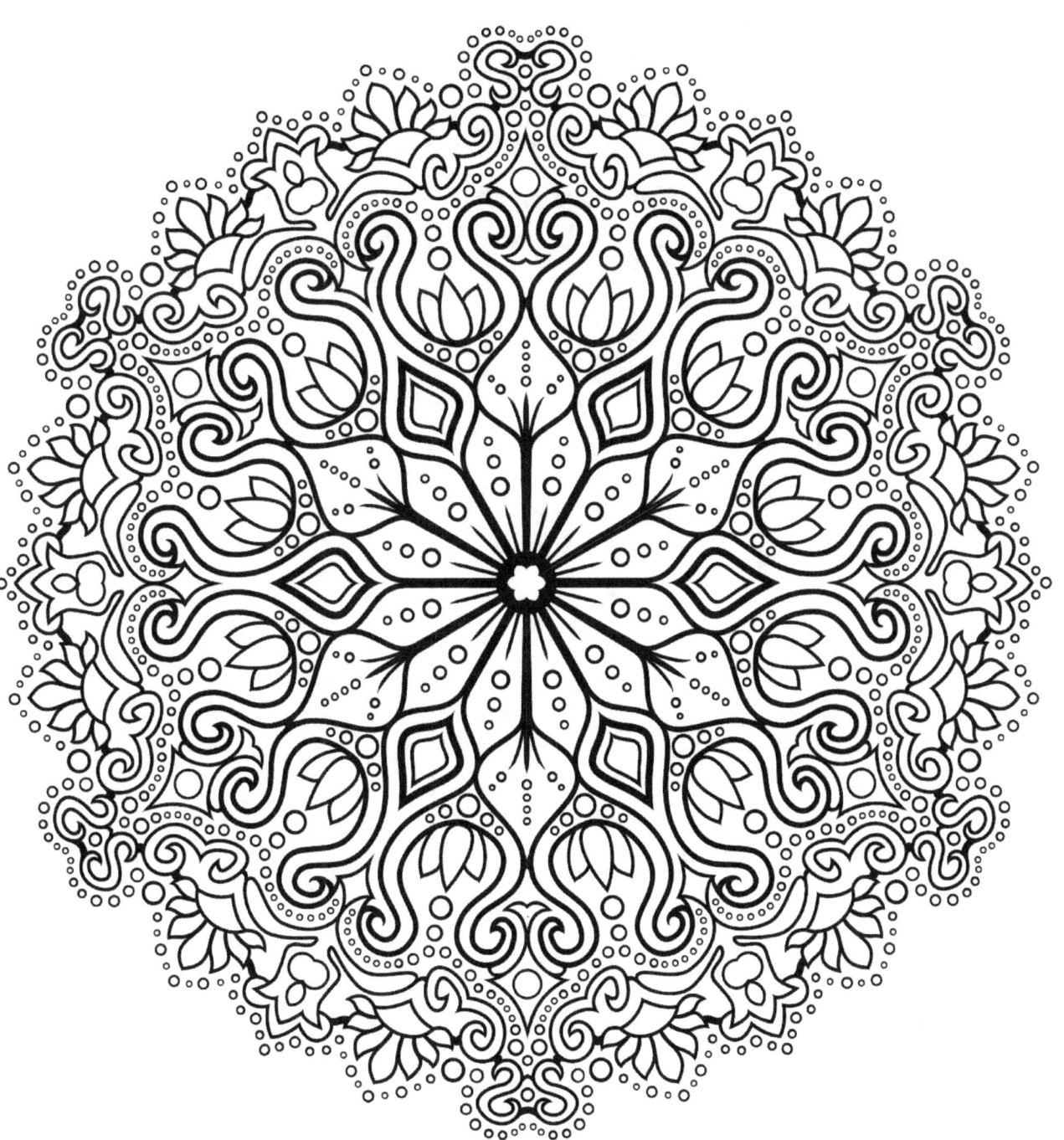

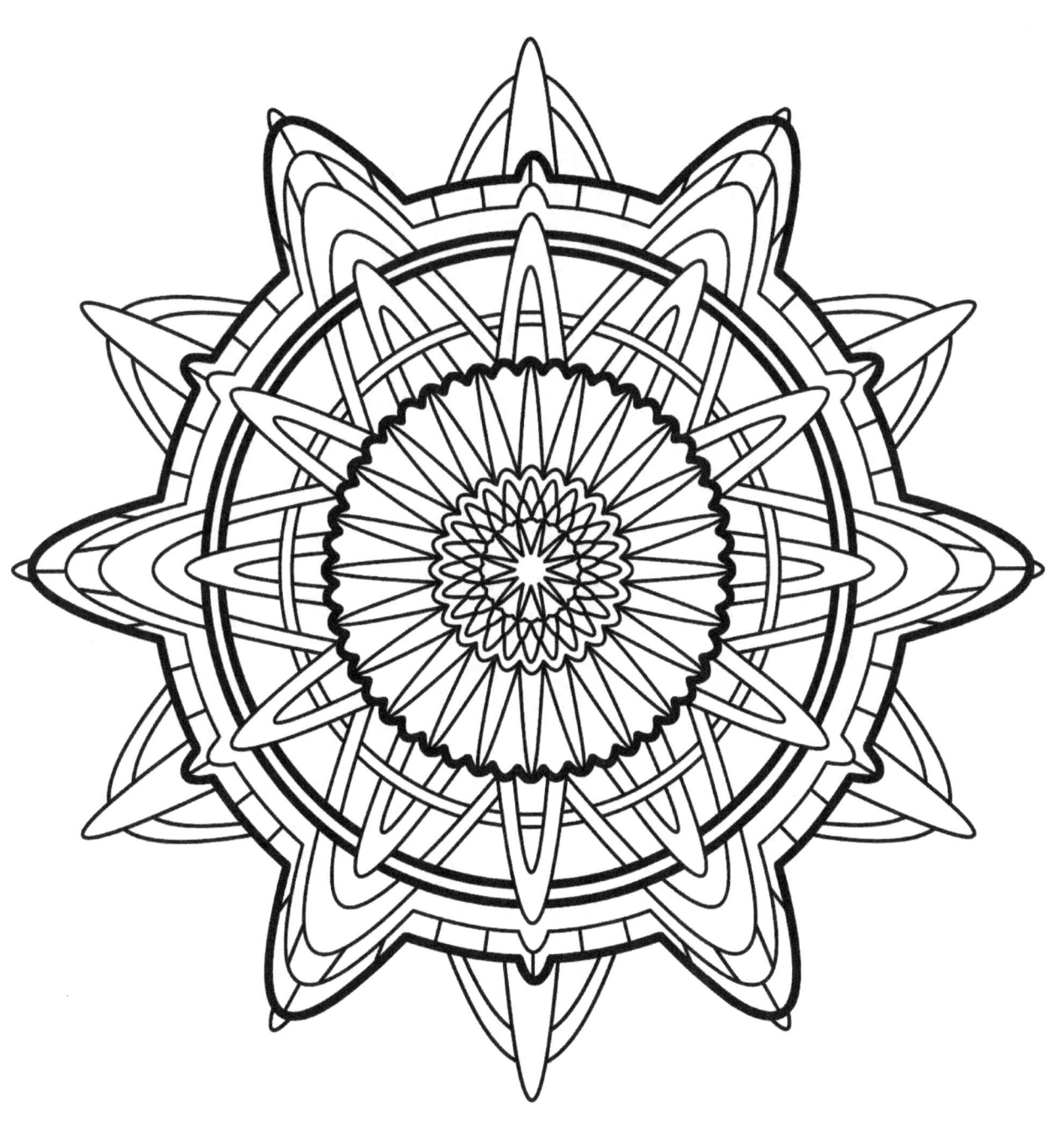

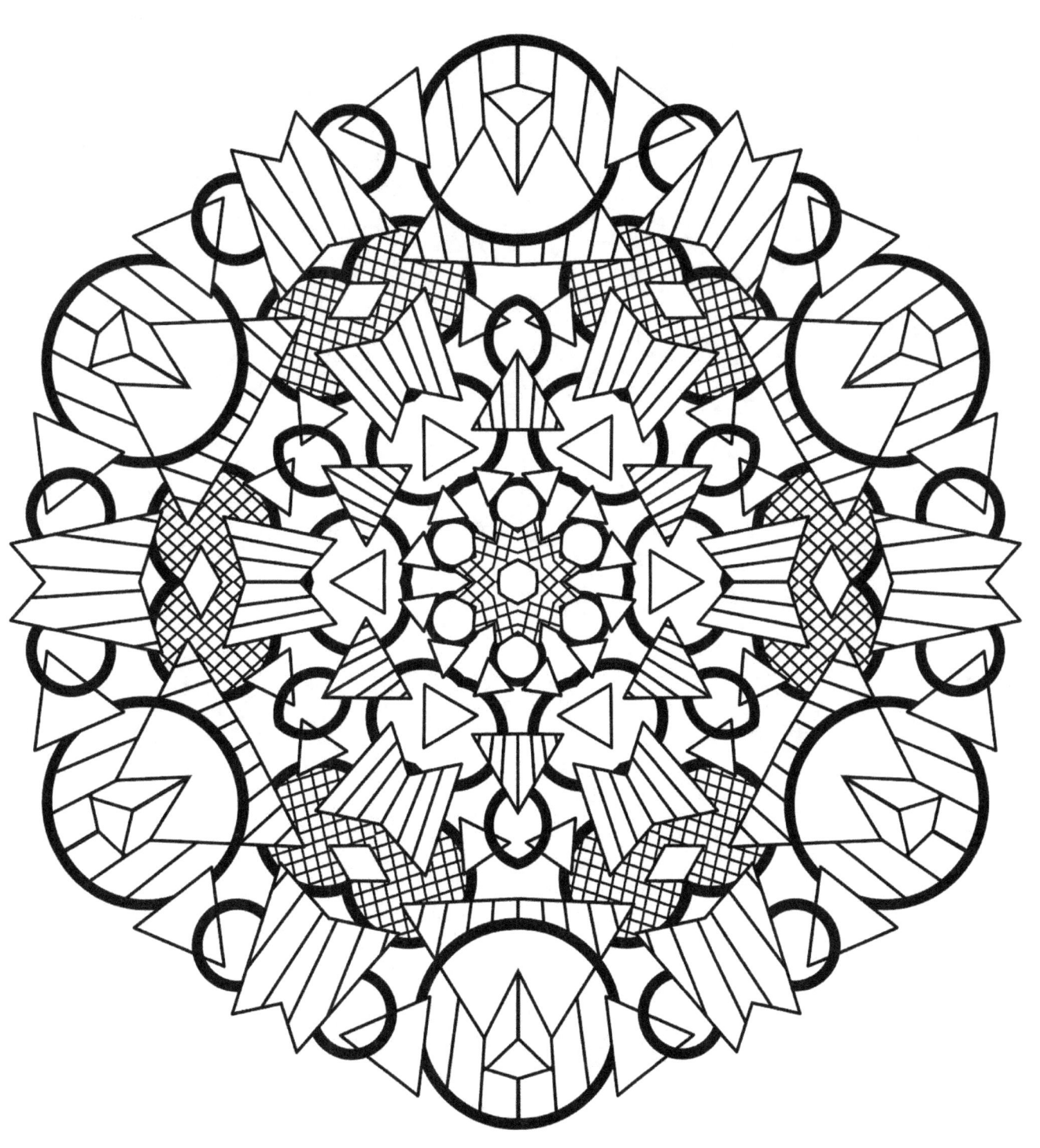

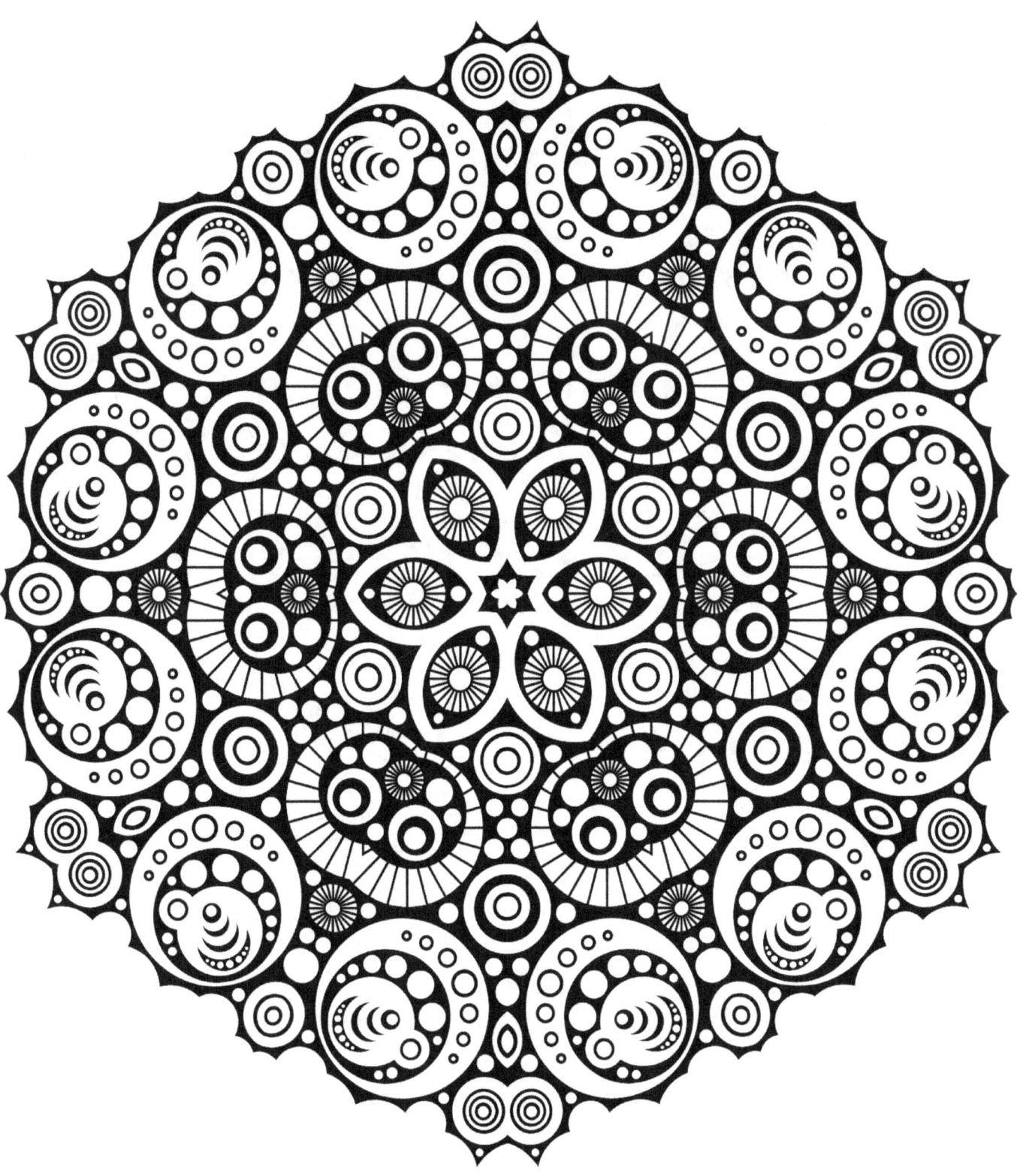

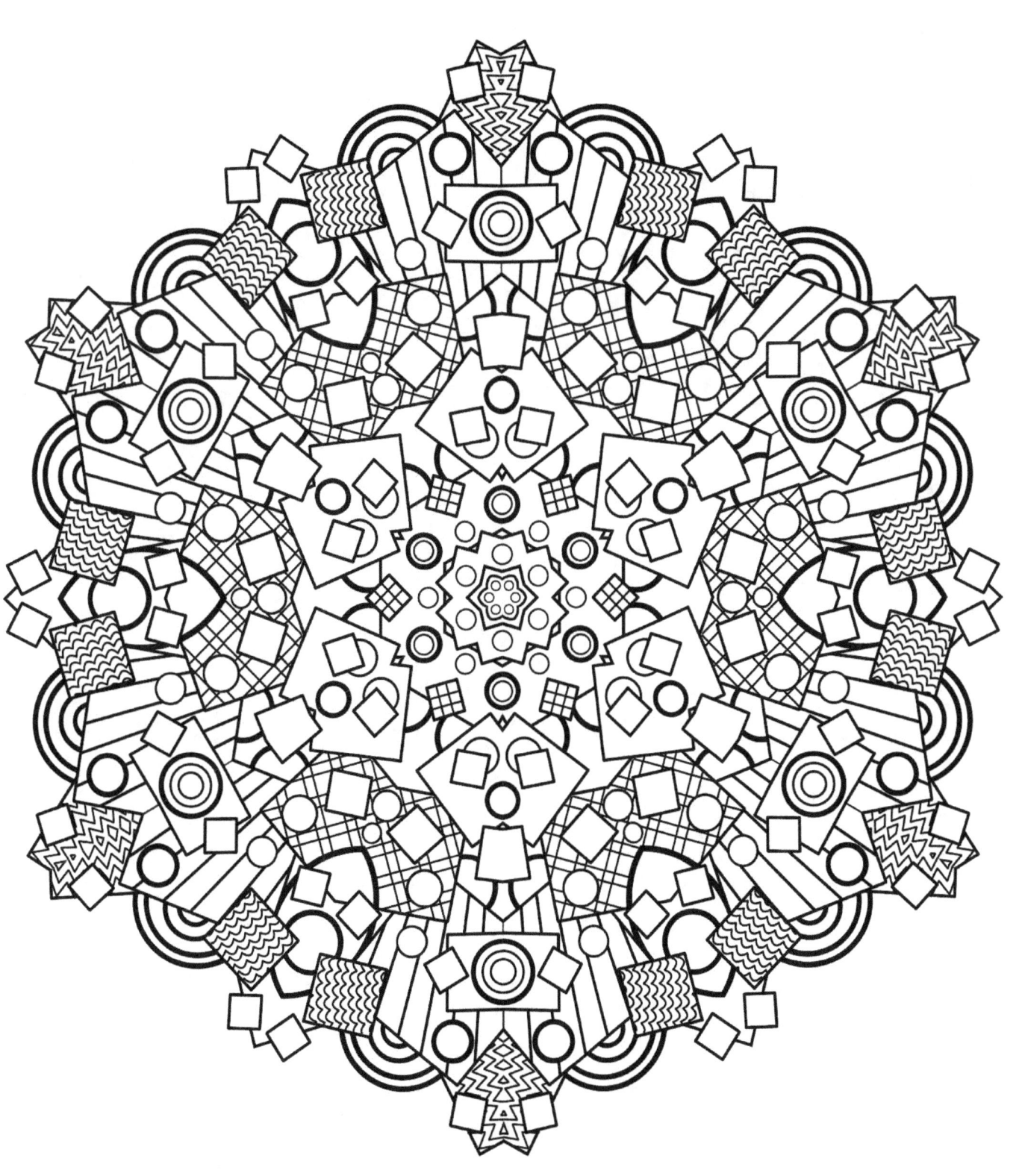

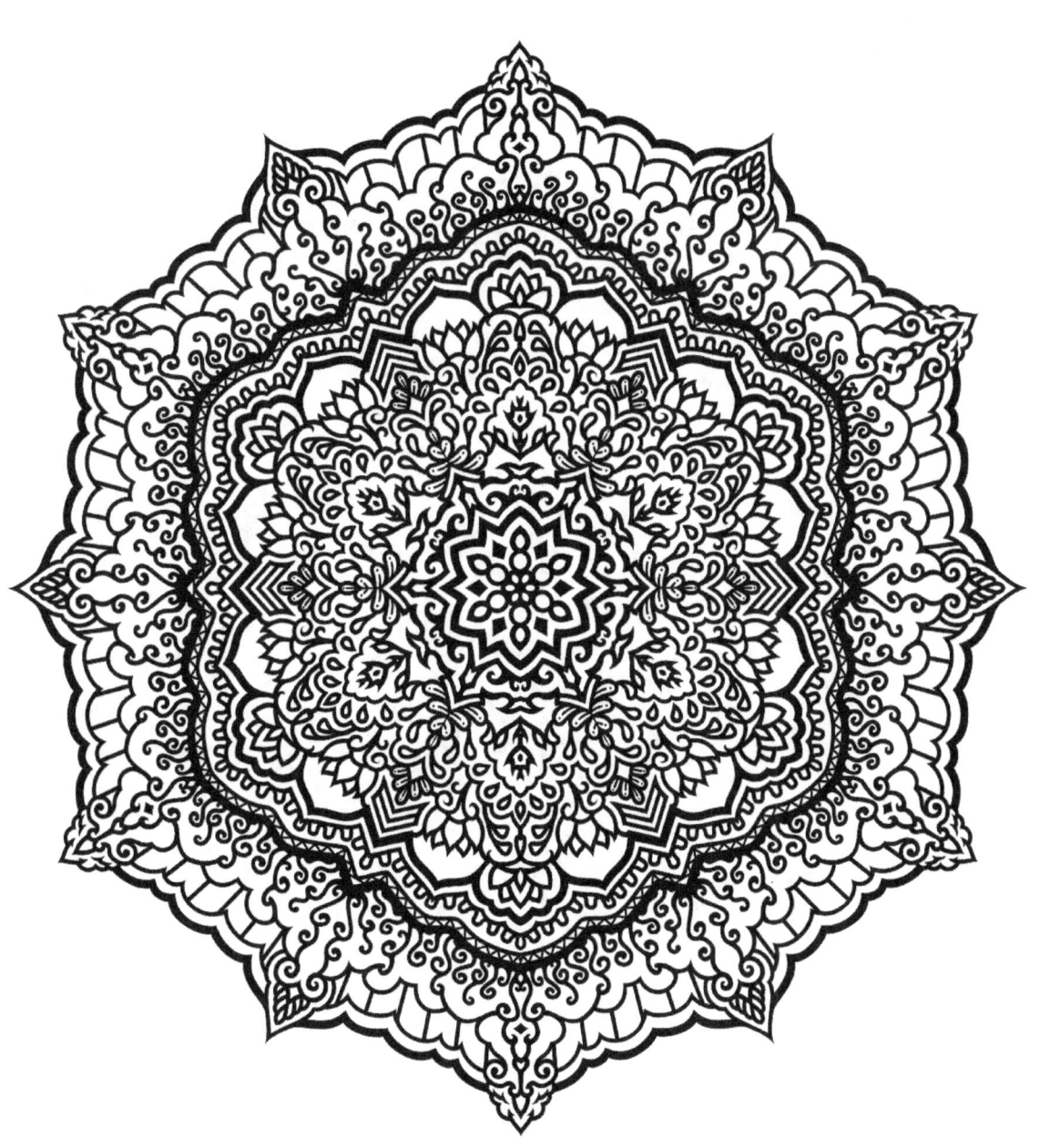

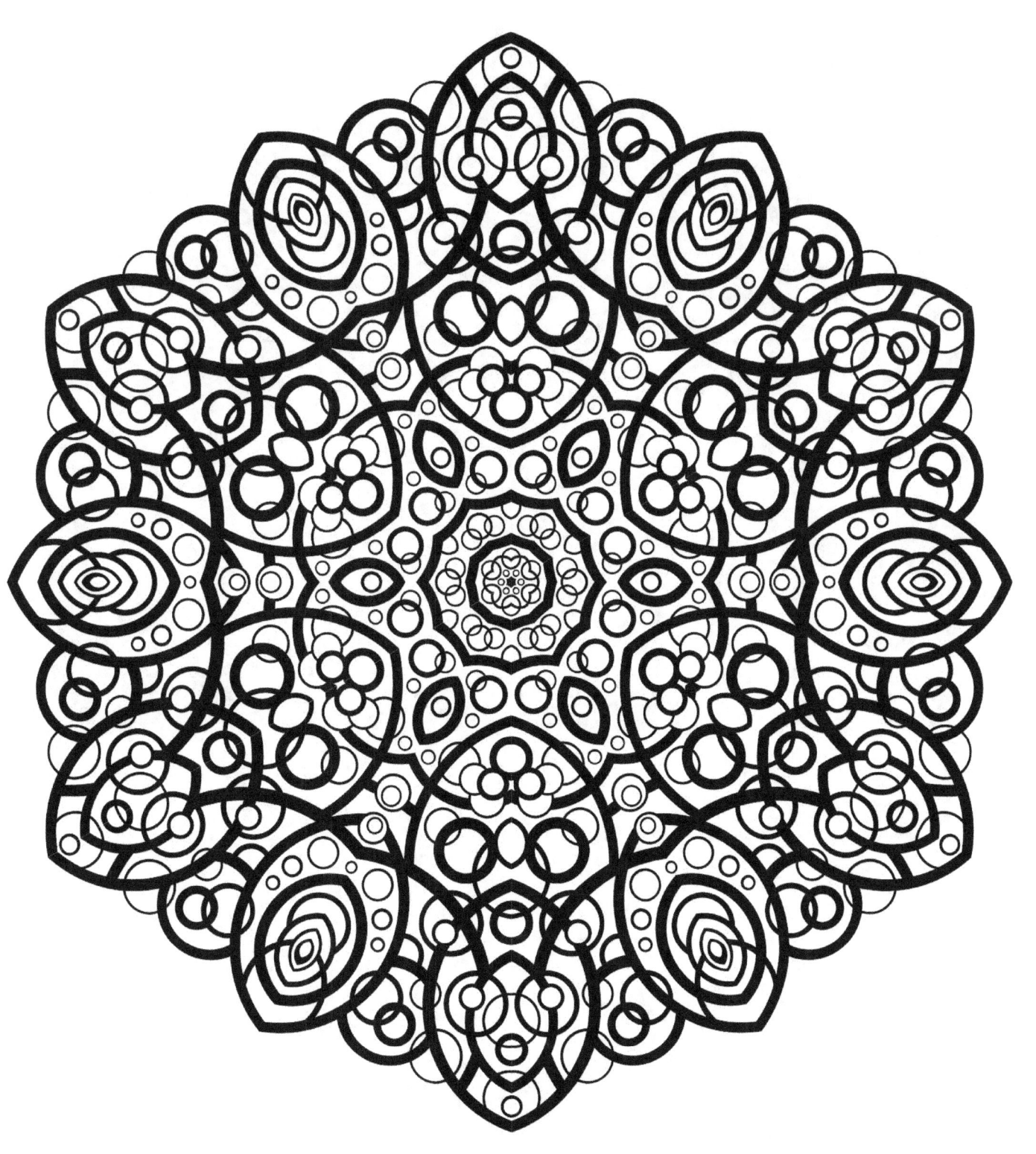

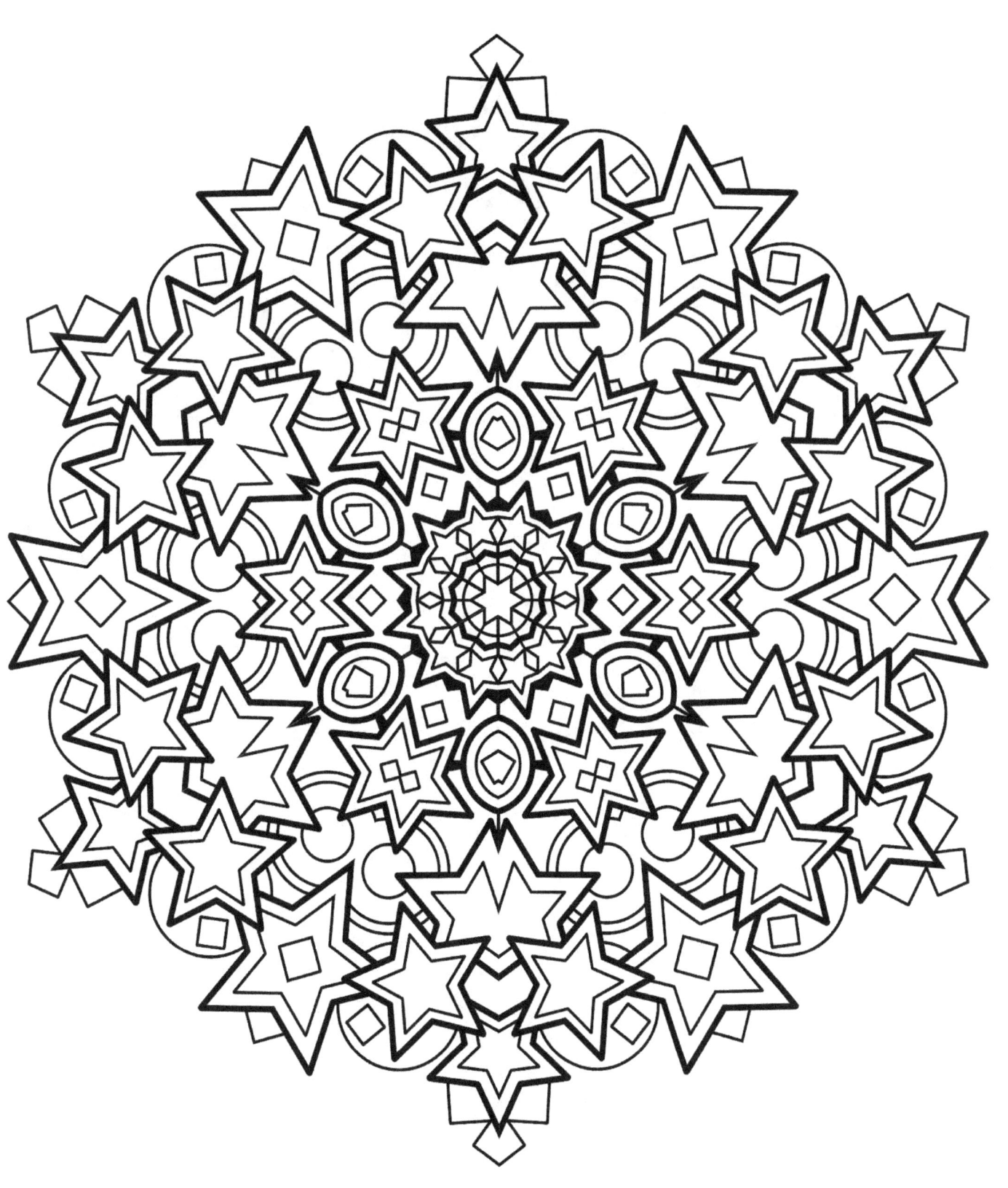

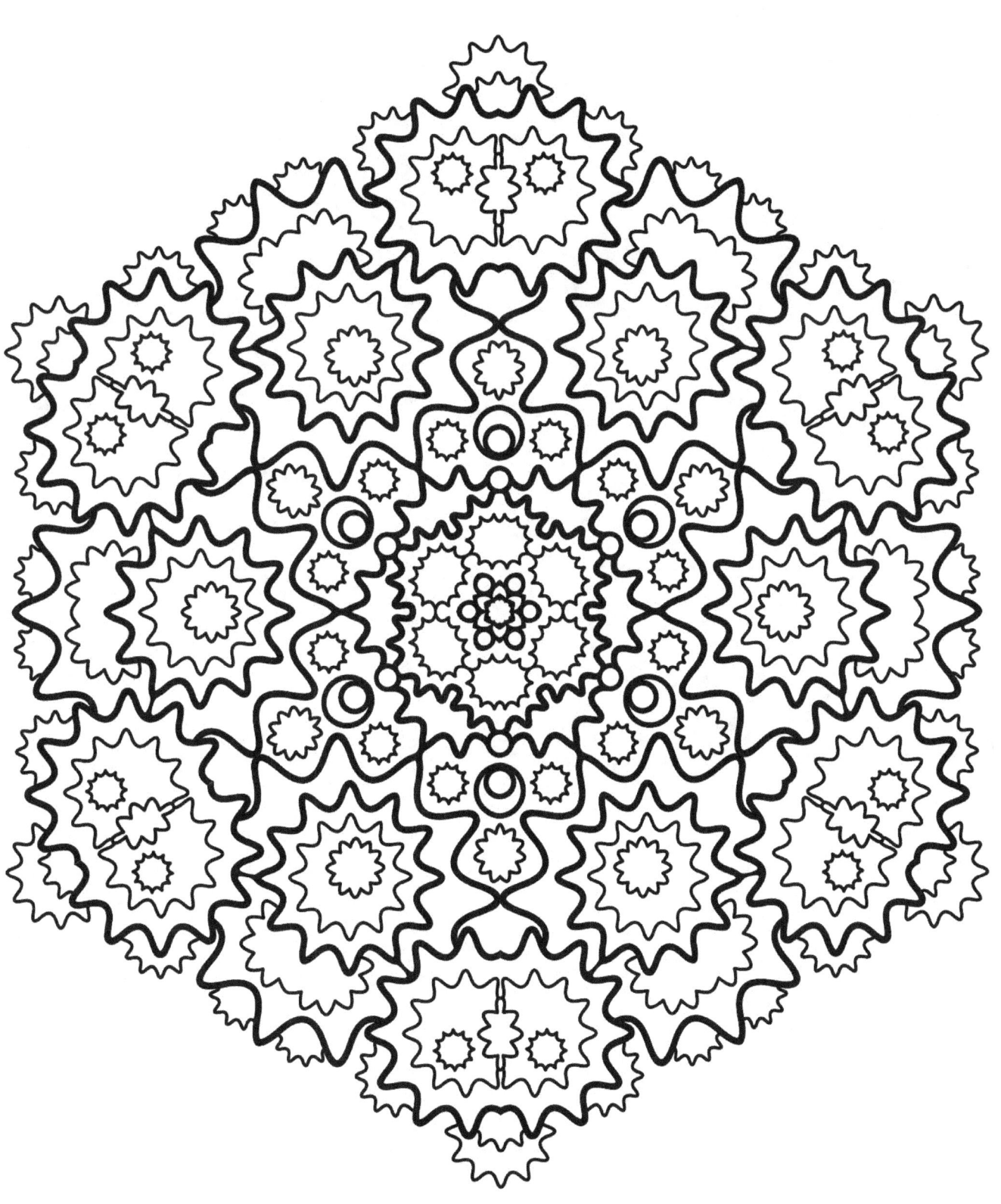

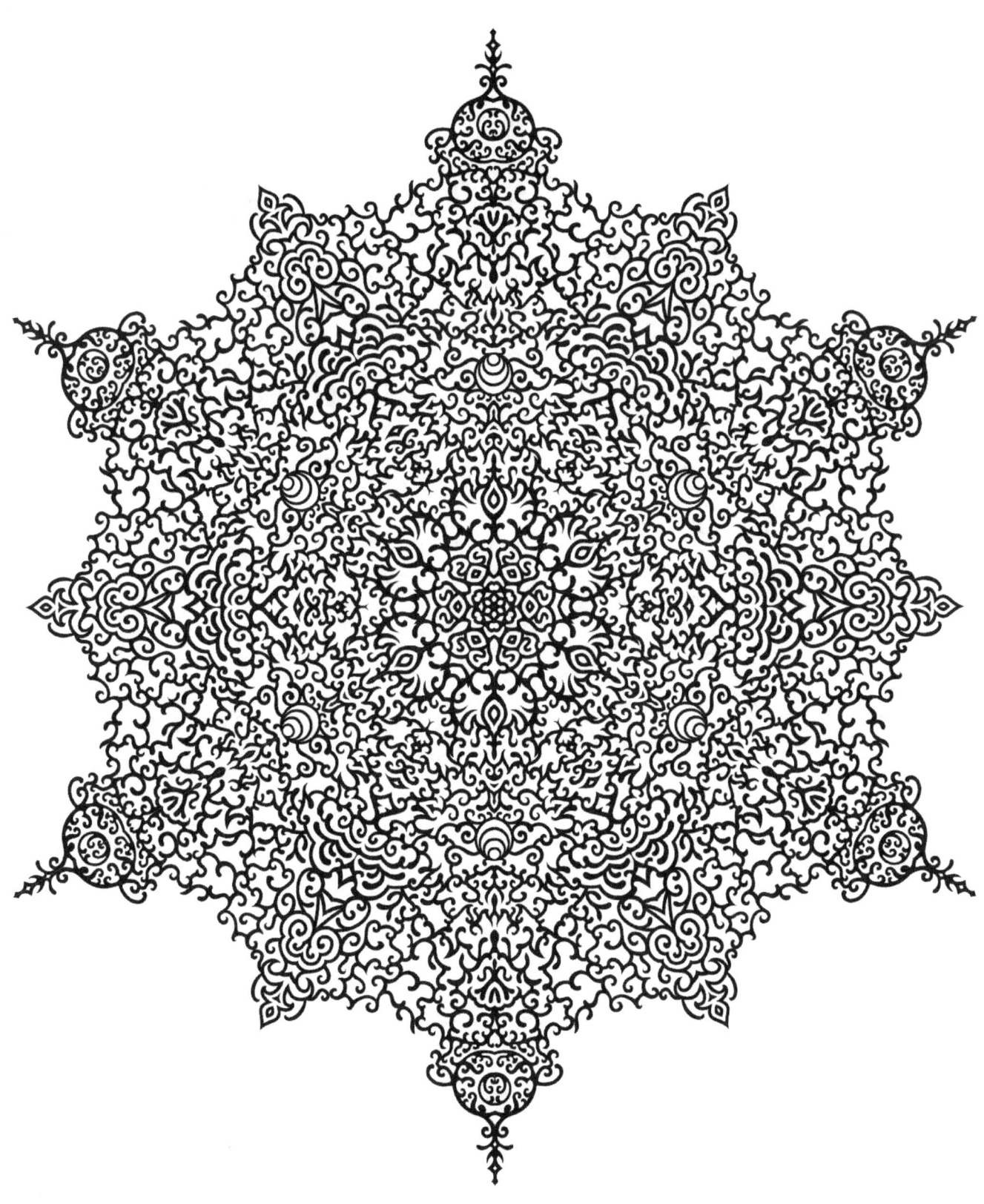

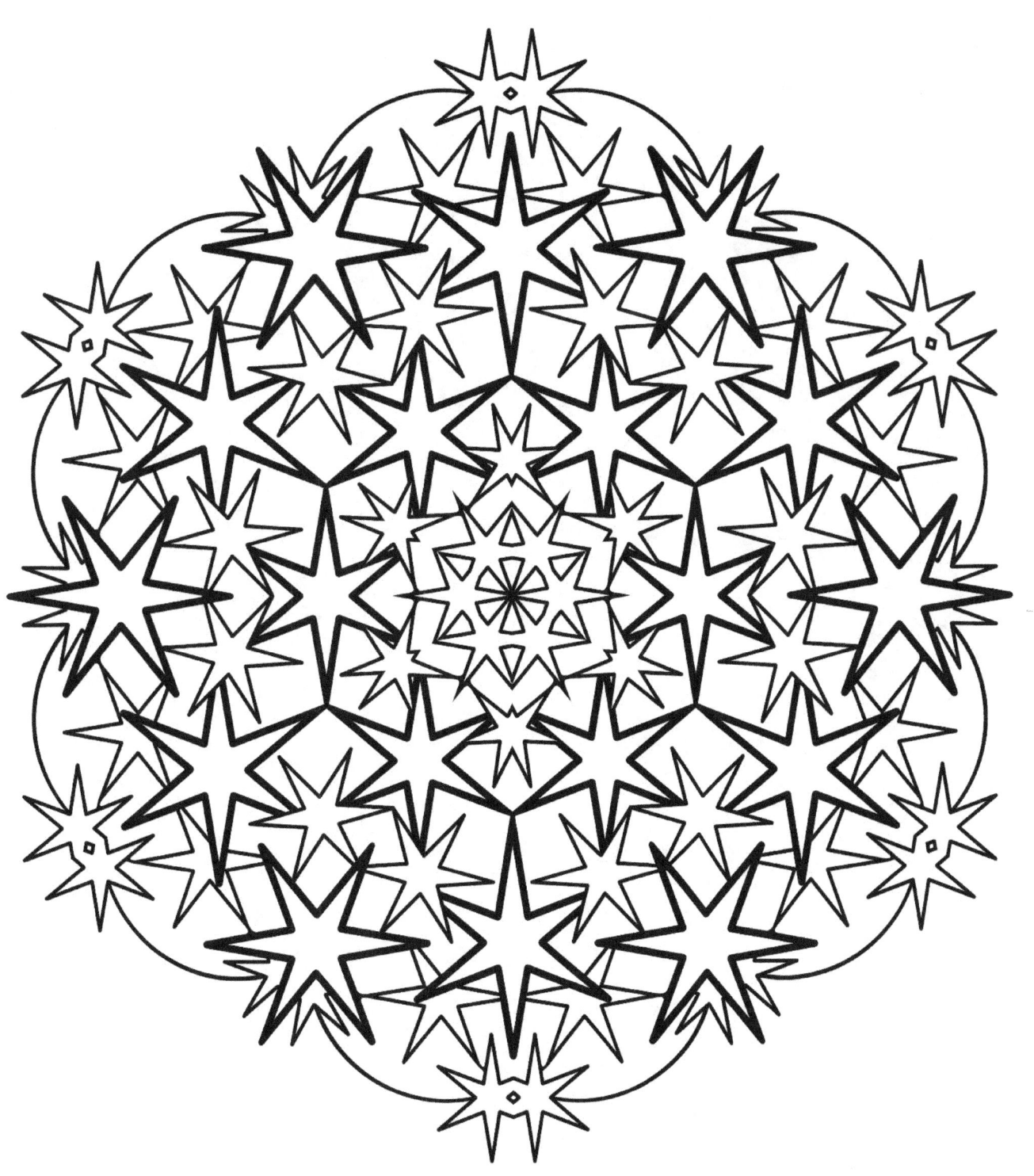

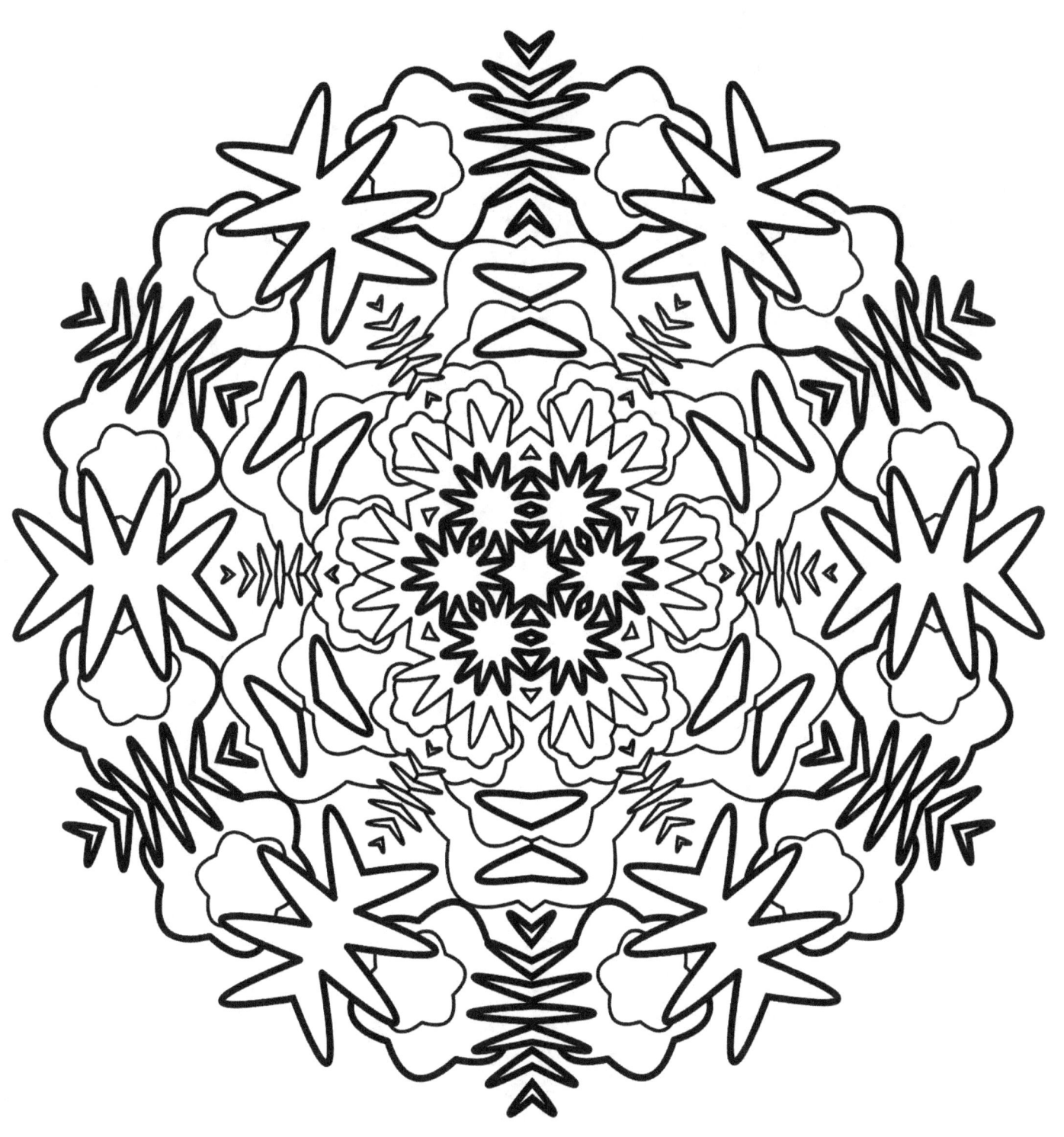

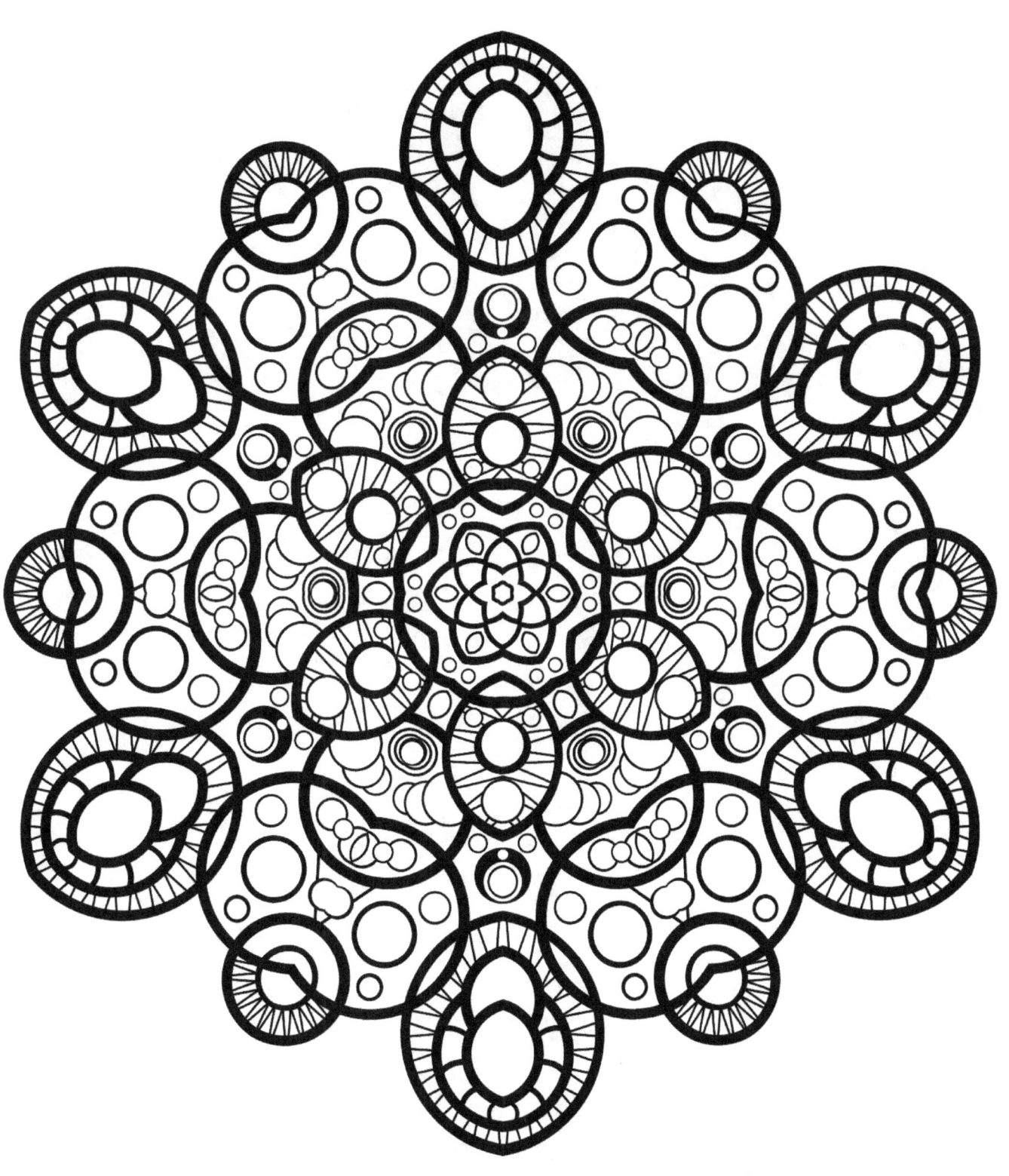

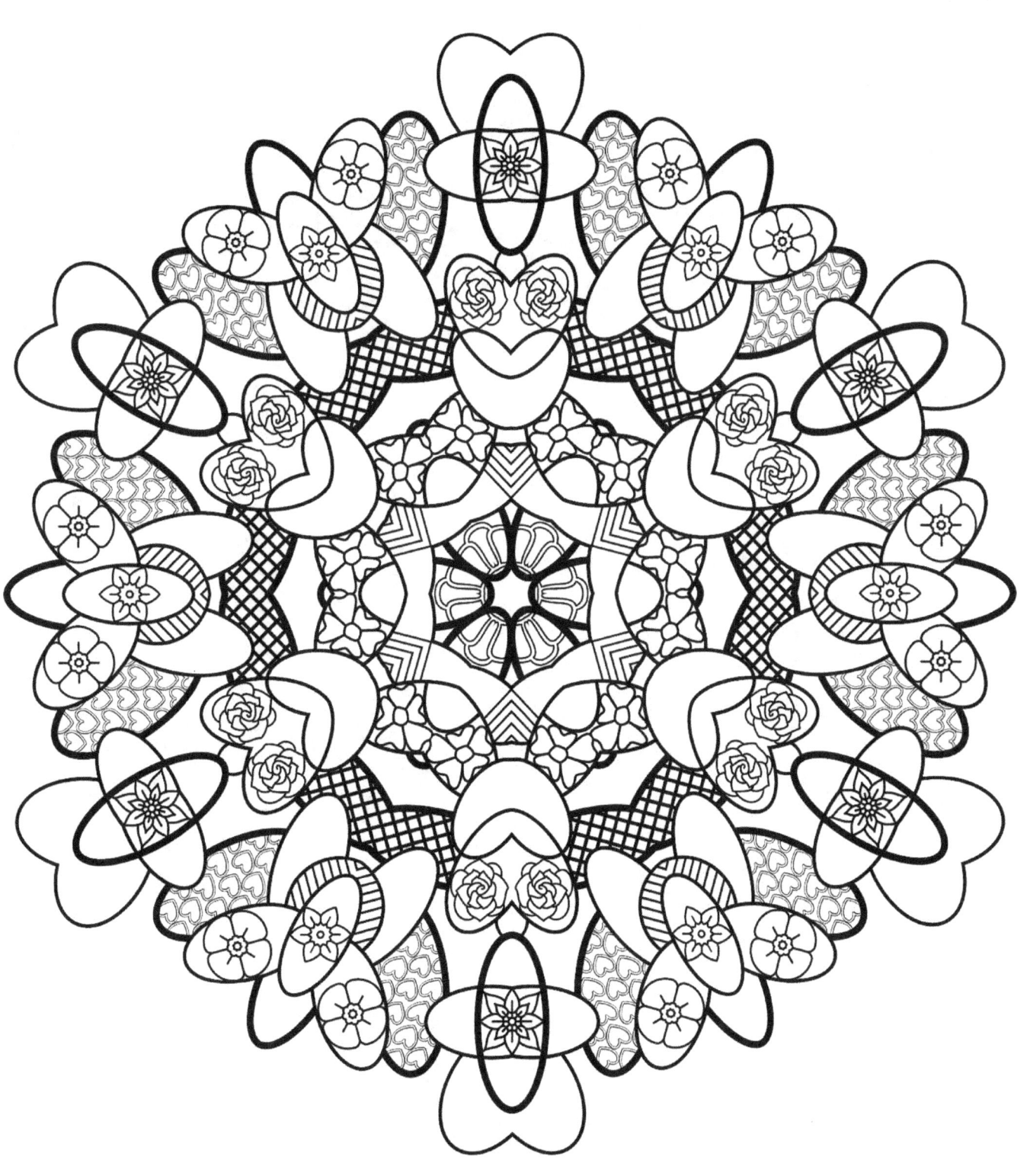

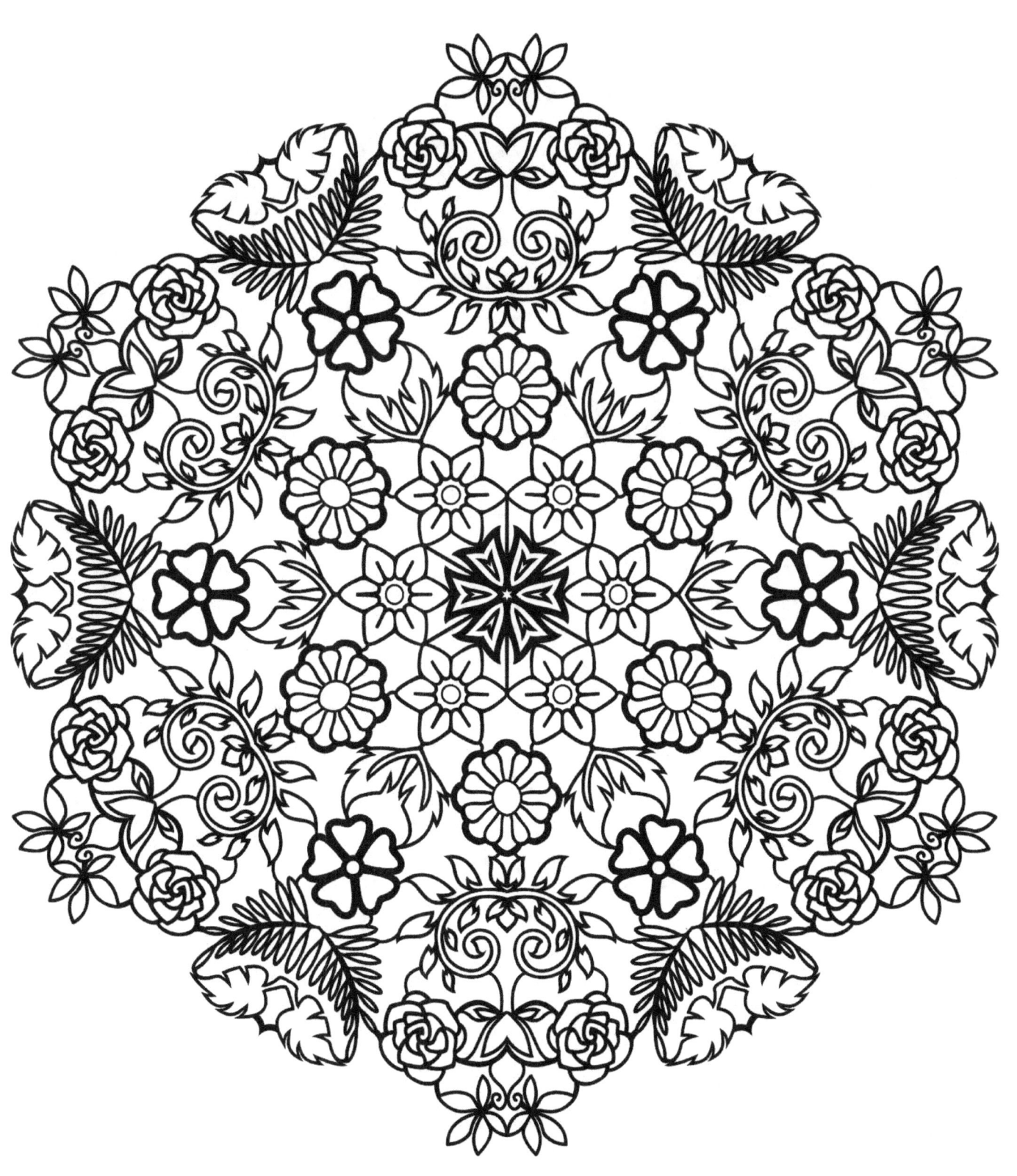

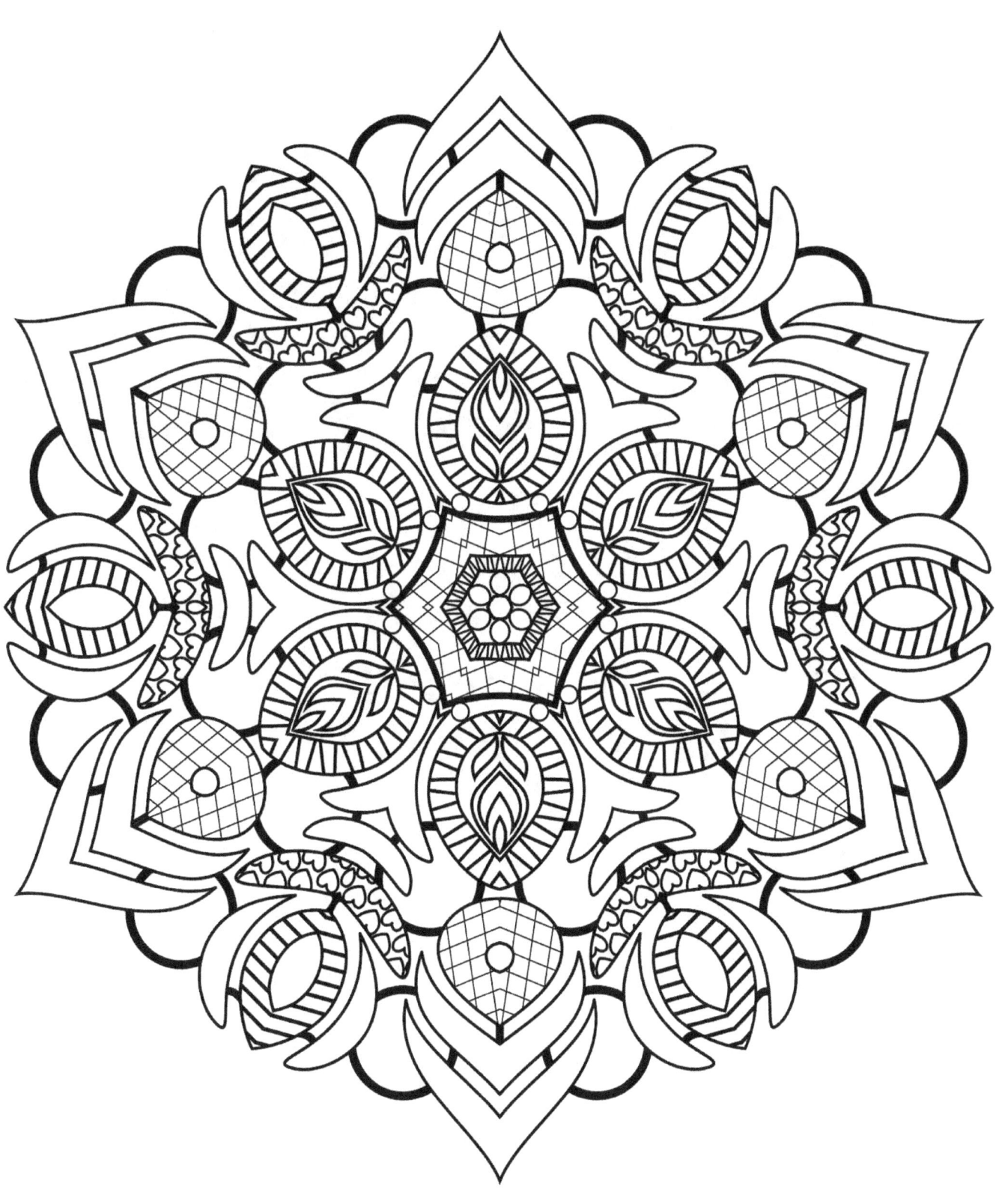

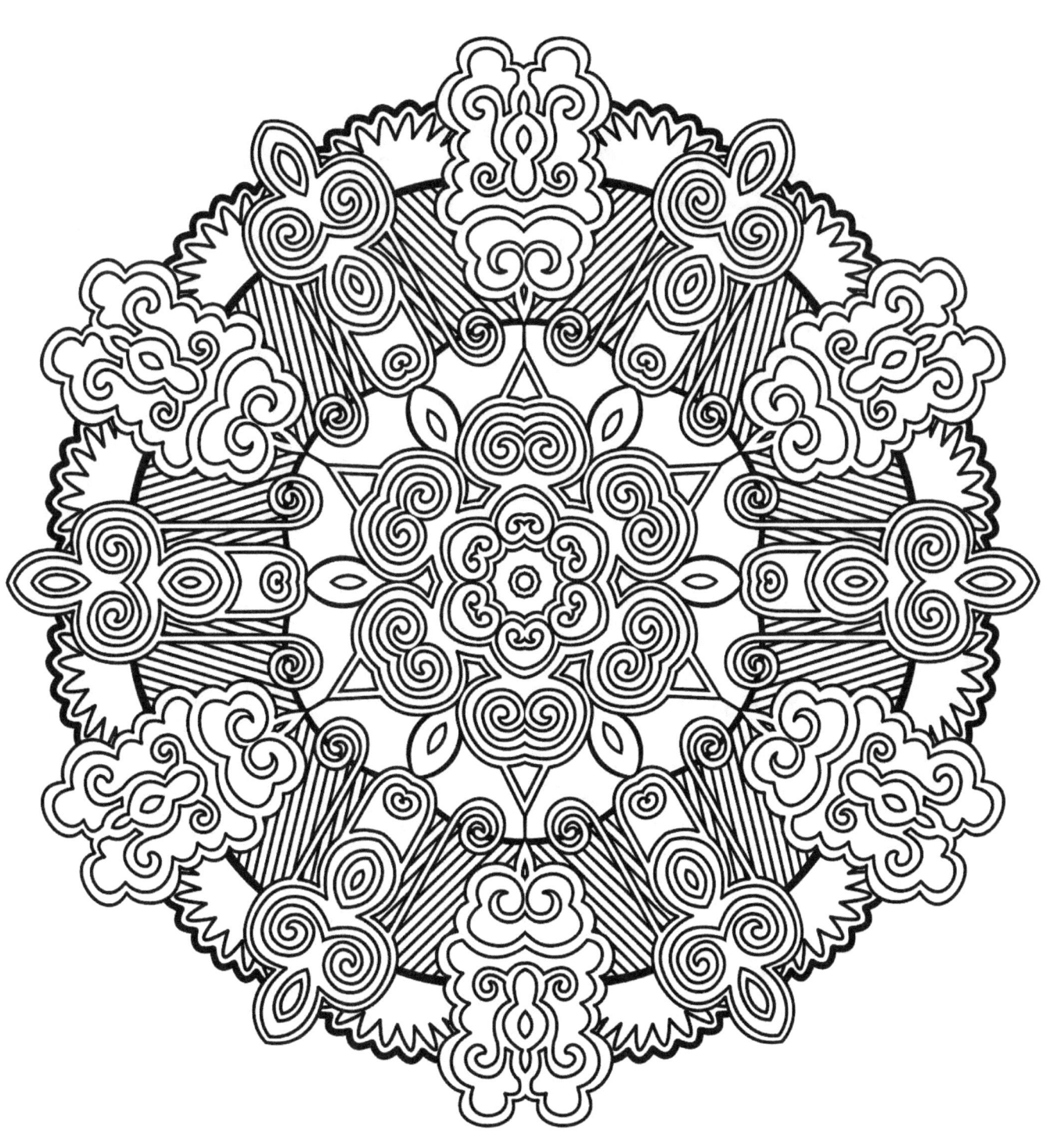

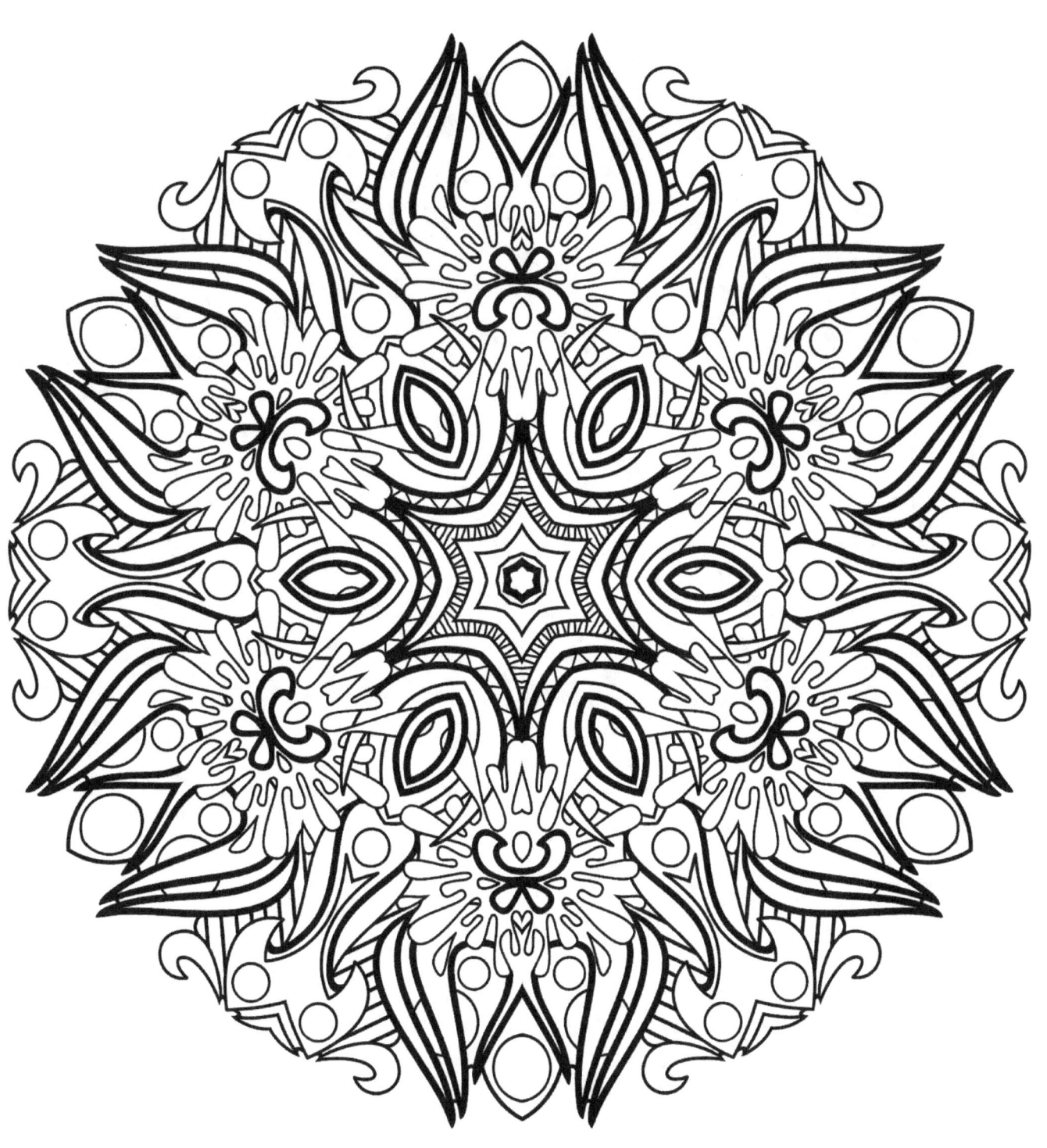

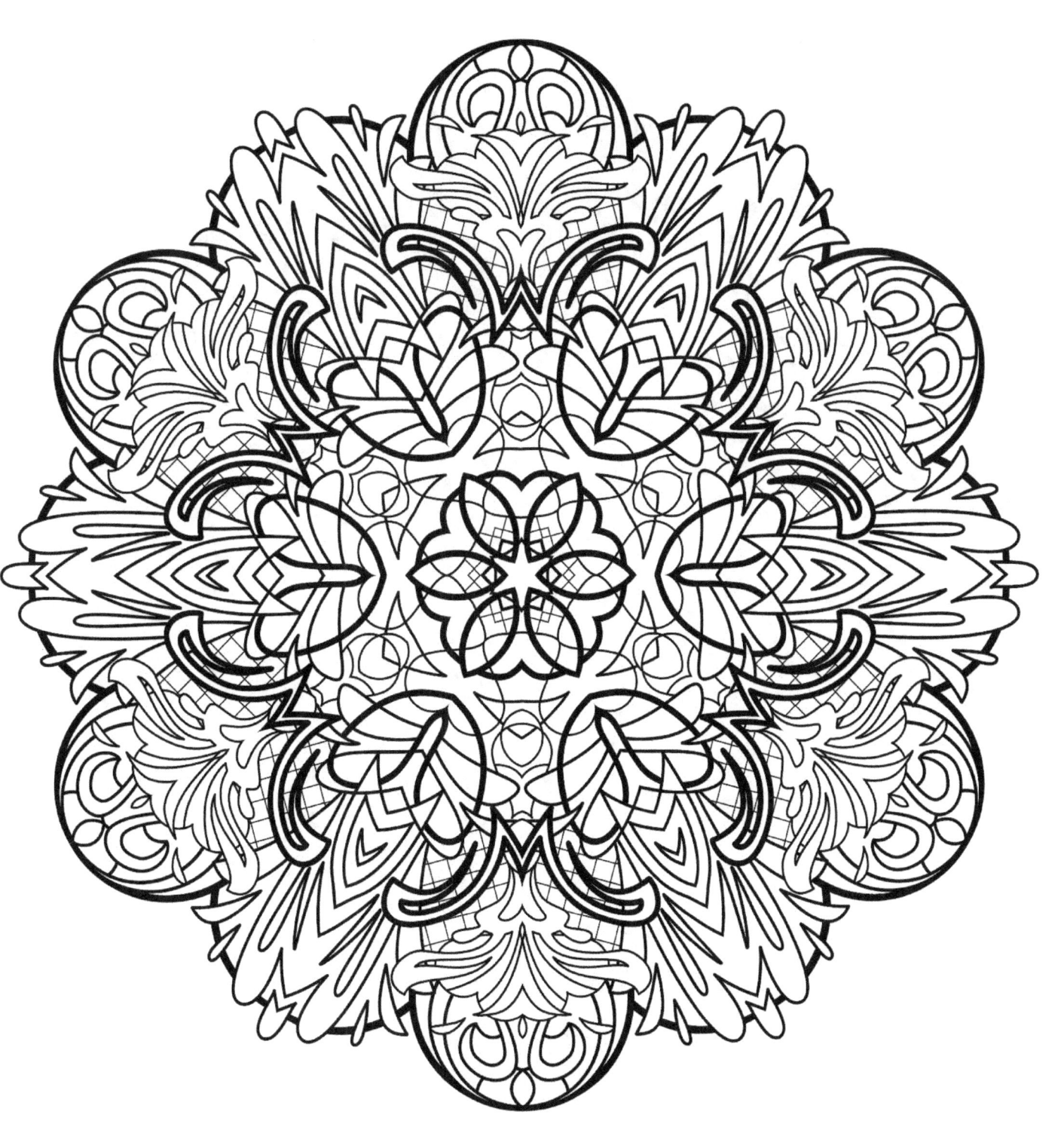

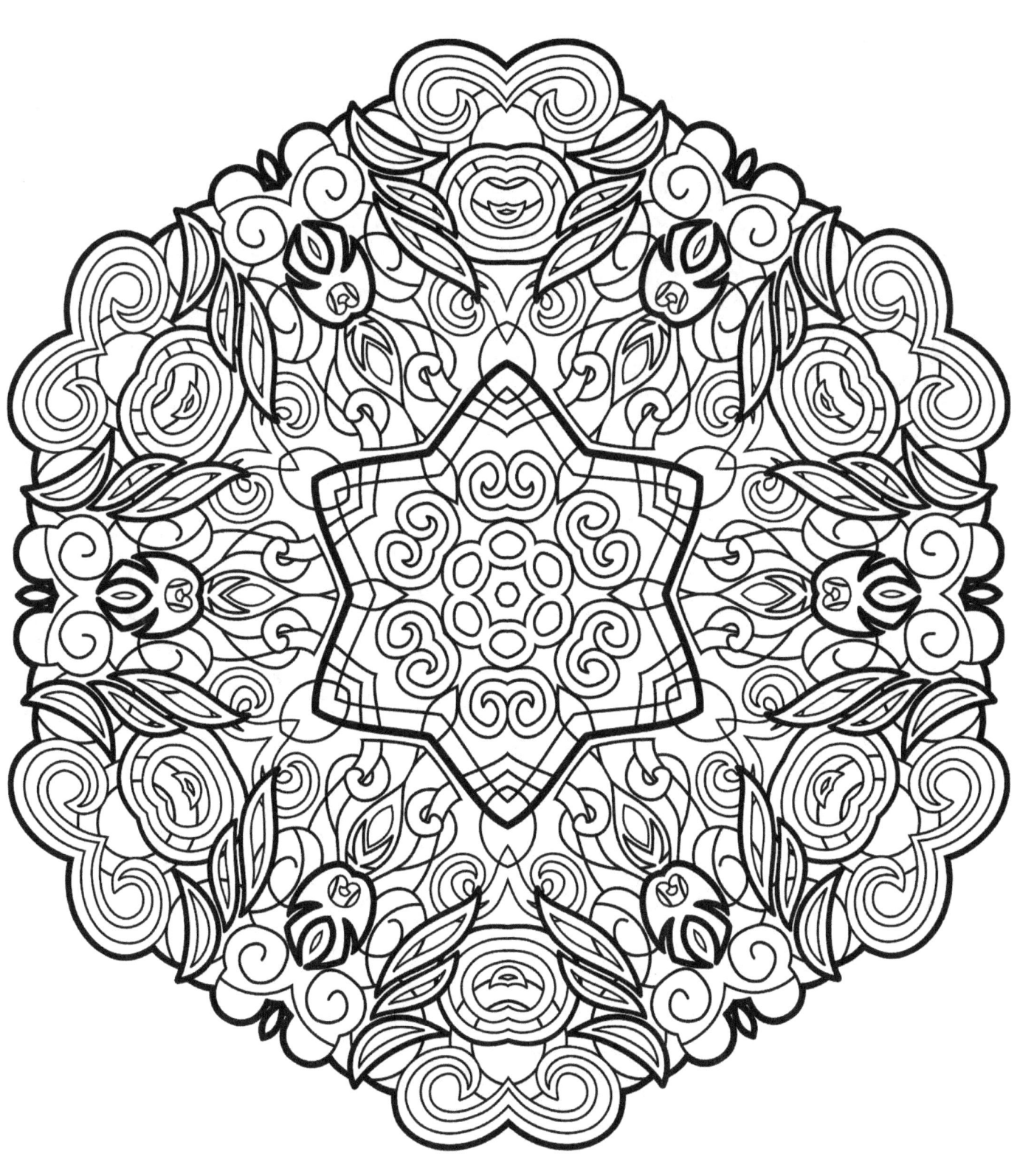

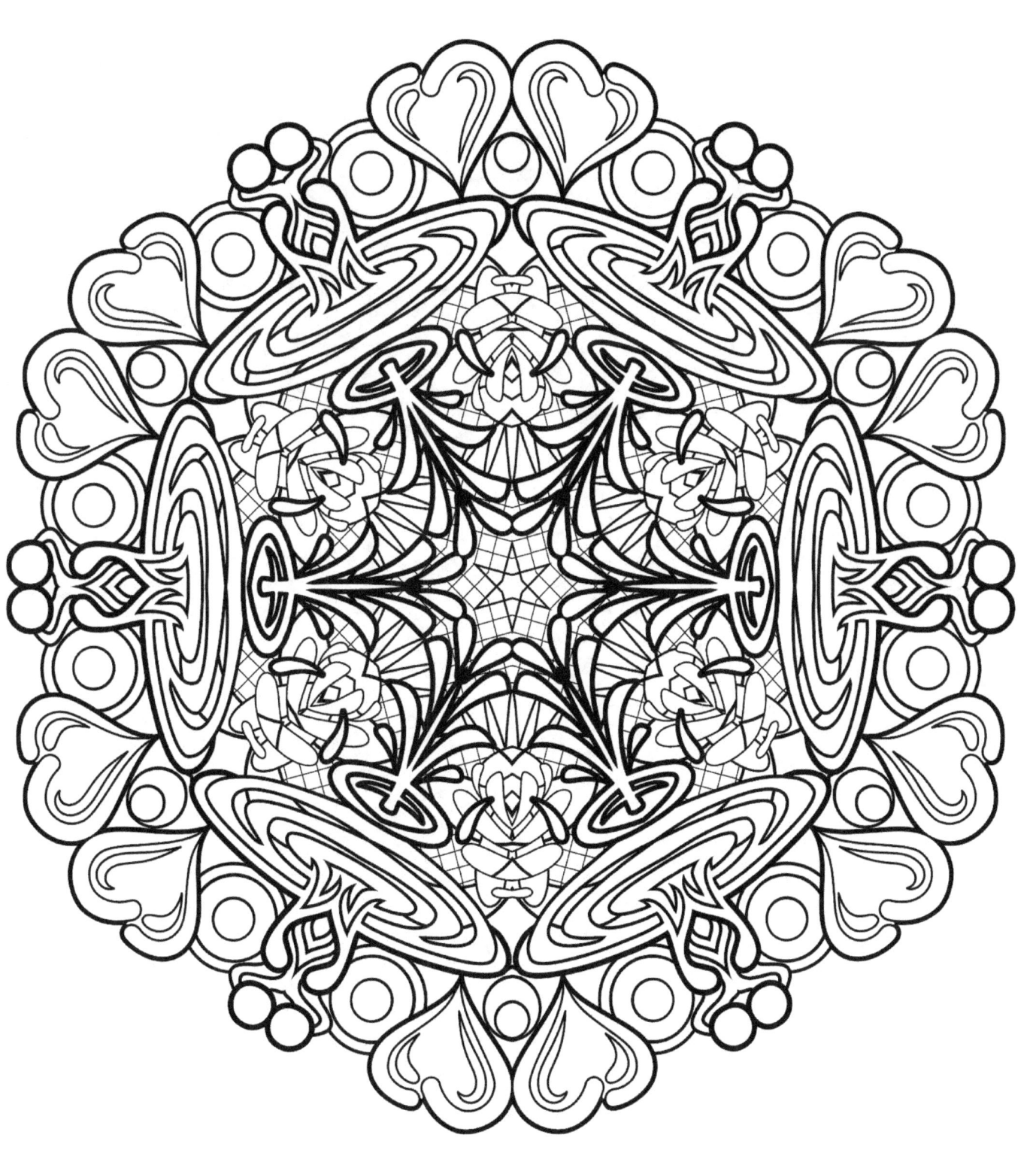

www.ingramcontent.com/pod-product-compliance
Lightning Source LLC
Chambersburg PA
CBHW080002230526
45470CB00008B/2833